FREDERICK THE GREAT

FREDERICK THE GREAT

Mary Kittredge

CHELSEA HOUSE PUBLISHERS
NEW YORK
NEW HAVEN   PHILADELPHIA

EDITOR-IN-CHIEF: Nancy Toff
EXECUTIVE EDITOR: Remmel T. Nunn
MANAGING EDITOR: Karyn Gullen Browne
COPY CHIEF: Perry Scott King
ART DIRECTOR: Giannella Garrett

Staff for FREDERICK THE GREAT:

SENIOR EDITOR: John W. Selfridge
ASSISTANT EDITORS: Maria Behan, Pierre Hauser, Kathleen McDermott, Bert Yaeger
COPY EDITORS: Gillian Bucky, Sean Dolan
DESIGN ASSISTANT: Jill Goldreyer
PICTURE RESEARCH: Diane Moroff
LAYOUT: David Murray
PRODUCTION COORDINATOR: Alma Rodriguez
COVER ILLUSTRATION: Michael Garland

CREATIVE DIRECTOR: Harold Steinberg

Frontispiece courtesy of The Bettmann Archive

3 5 7 9 8 6 4 2

Library of Congress Cataloging in Publication Data

Kittredge, Mary. FREDERICK THE GREAT

(World leaders past & present)
Bibliography: p. 108
Includes index.
1. Frederick II, King of Prussia, 1712–1786—Juvenile
literature. 2. Prussia (Germany)—Kings and rulers—
Biography—Juvenile literature. 3. Prussia (Germany)—
History—Frederick II, the Great, 1740–1786—Juvenile
literature. [1. Frederick II, King of Prussia, 1712–86.
2. Kings, queens, rulers, etc. 3. Prussia (Germany)—
History—Frederick II, the Great, 1740–1786] I. Title.
II. Series.
DD404.K58   1987   943.053′092′4 [B] [92]
86-32693

ISBN 0-87754-525-1

Contents

"On Leadership," Arthur M. Schlesinger, jr. 7

1. A King and His Courage 13
2. Raised to Be King 25
3. The Young Philosopher-King 41
4. Rendezvous with Glory 53
5. The Rising Tempest 73
6. The Enlightened Absolutist 91

Further Reading 108
Chronology 109
Index 110

CHELSEA HOUSE PUBLISHERS

WORLD LEADERS PAST & PRESENT

ADENAUER	FREDERICK THE GREAT	MARY, QUEEN OF SCOTS
ALEXANDER THE GREAT	INDIRA GANDHI	GOLDA MEIR
MARC ANTONY	MOHANDAS GANDHI	METTERNICH
KING ARTHUR	GARIBALDI	MUSSOLINI
ATATÜRK	GENGHIS KHAN	NAPOLEON
ATTLEE	GLADSTONE	NASSER
BEGIN	GORBACHEV	NEHRU
BEN-GURION	HAMMARSKJÖLD	NERO
BISMARCK	HENRY VIII	NICHOLAS II
LÉON BLUM	HENRY OF NAVARRE	NIXON
BOLÍVAR	HINDENBURG	NKRUMAH
CESARE BORGIA	HITLER	PERICLES
BRANDT	HO CHI MINH	PERÓN
BREZHNEV	HUSSEIN	QADDAFI
CAESAR	IVAN THE TERRIBLE	ROBESPIERRE
CALVIN	ANDREW JACKSON	ELEANOR ROOSEVELT
CASTRO	JEFFERSON	FRANKLIN D. ROOSEVELT
CATHERINE THE GREAT	JOAN OF ARC	THEODORE ROOSEVELT
CHARLEMAGNE	POPE JOHN XXIII	SADAT
CHIANG KAI-SHEK	LYNDON JOHNSON	STALIN
CHURCHILL	JUÁREZ	SUN YAT-SEN
CLEMENCEAU	JOHN F. KENNEDY	TAMERLANE
CLEOPATRA	KENYATTA	THATCHER
CORTÉS	KHOMEINI	TITO
CROMWELL	KHRUSHCHEV	TROTSKY
DANTON	MARTIN LUTHER KING, JR.	TRUDEAU
DE GAULLE	KISSINGER	TRUMAN
DE VALERA	LENIN	VICTORIA
DISRAELI	LINCOLN	WASHINGTON
EISENHOWER	LLOYD GEORGE	WEIZMANN
ELEANOR OF AQUITAINE	LOUIS XIV	WOODROW WILSON
QUEEN ELIZABETH I	LUTHER	XERXES
FERDINAND AND ISABELLA	JUDAS MACCABEUS	ZHOU ENLAI
FRANCO	MAO ZEDONG	

ON LEADERSHIP
Arthur M. Schlesinger, jr.

LEADERSHIP, it may be said, is really what makes the world go round. Love no doubt smooths the passage; but love is a private transaction between consenting adults. Leadership is a public transaction with history. The idea of leadership affirms the capacity of individuals to move, inspire, and mobilize masses of people so that they act together in pursuit of an end. Sometimes leadership serves good purposes, sometimes bad; but whether the end is benign or evil, great leaders are those men and women who leave their personal stamp on history.

Now, the very concept of leadership implies the proposition that individuals can make a difference. This proposition has never been universally accepted. From classical times to the present day, eminent thinkers have regarded individuals as no more than the agents and pawns of larger forces, whether the gods and goddesses of the ancient world or, in the modern era, race, class, nation, the dialectic, the will of the people, the spirit of the times, history itself. Against such forces, the individual dwindles into insignificance.

So contends the thesis of historical determinism. Tolstoy's great novel *War and Peace* offers a famous statement of the case. Why, Tolstoy asked, did millions of men in the Napoleonic wars, denying their human feelings and their common sense, move back and forth across Europe slaughtering their fellows? "The war," Tolstoy answered, "was bound to happen simply because it was bound to happen." All prior history predetermined it. As for leaders, they, Tolstoy said, "are but the labels that serve to give a name to an end and, like labels, they have the least possible connection with the event." The greater the leader, "the more conspicuous the inevitability and the predestination of every act he commits." The leader, said Tolstoy, is "the slave of history."

Determinism takes many forms. Marxism is the determinism of class. Nazism the determinism of race. But the idea of men and women as the slaves of history runs athwart the deepest human instincts. Rigid determinism abolishes the idea of human freedom—

the assumption of free choice that underlies every move we make, every word we speak, every thought we think. It abolishes the idea of human responsibility, since it is manifestly unfair to reward or punish people for actions that are by definition beyond their control. No one can live consistently by any deterministic creed. The Marxist states prove this themselves by their extreme susceptibility to the cult of leadership.

More than that, history refutes the idea that individuals make no difference. In December 1931 a British politician crossing Park Avenue in New York City between 76th and 77th Streets around 10:30 P.M. looked in the wrong direction and was knocked down by an automobile—a moment, he later recalled, of a man aghast, a world aglare: "I do not understand why I was not broken like an eggshell or squashed like a gooseberry." Fourteen months later an American politician, sitting in an open car in Miami, Florida, was fired on by an assassin; the man beside him was hit. Those who believe that individuals make no difference to history might well ponder whether the next two decades would have been the same had Mario Constasino's car killed Winston Churchill in 1931 and Giuseppe Zangara's bullet killed Franklin Roosevelt in 1933. Suppose, in addition, that Adolf Hitler had been killed in the street fighting during the Munich *Putsch* of 1923 and that Lenin had died of typhus during World War I. What would the 20th century be like now?

For better or for worse, individuals do make a difference. "The notion that a people can run itself and its affairs anonymously," wrote the philosopher William James, "is now well known to be the silliest of absurdities. Mankind does nothing save through initiatives on the part of inventors, great or small, and imitation by the rest of us—these are the sole factors in human progress. Individuals of genius show the way, and set the patterns, which common people then adopt and follow."

Leadership, James suggests, means leadership in thought as well as in action. In the long run, leaders in thought may well make the greater difference to the world. But, as Woodrow Wilson once said, "Those only are leaders of men, in the general eye, who lead in action. . . . It is at their hands that new thought gets its translation into the crude language of deeds." Leaders in thought often invent in solitude and obscurity, leaving to later generations the tasks of imitation. Leaders in action—the leaders portrayed in this series—have to be effective in their own time.

And they cannot be effective by themselves. They must act in response to the rhythms of their age. Their genius must be adapted, in a phrase of William James's, "to the receptivities of the moment." Leaders are useless without followers. "There goes the mob," said the French politician hearing a clamor in the streets. "I am their leader. I must follow them." Great leaders turn the inchoate emotions of the mob to purposes of their own. They seize on the opportunities of their time, the hopes, fears, frustrations, crises, potentialities. They succeed when events have prepared the way for them, when the community is awaiting to be aroused, when they can provide the clarifying and organizing ideas. Leadership ignites the circuit between the individual and the mass and thereby alters history.

It may alter history for better or for worse. Leaders have been responsible for the most extravagant follies and most monstrous crimes that have beset suffering humanity. They have also been vital in such gains as humanity has made in individual freedom, religious and racial tolerance, social justice and respect for human rights.

There is no sure way to tell in advance who is going to lead for good and who for evil. But a glance at the gallery of men and women in *World Leaders—Past and Present* suggests some useful tests.

One test is this: do leaders lead by force or by persuasion? By command or by consent? Through most of history leadership was exercised by the divine right of authority. The duty of followers was to defer and to obey. "Theirs not to reason why,/ Theirs but to do and die." On occasion, as with the so-called "enlightened despots" of the 18th century in Europe, absolutist leadership was animated by humane purposes. More often, absolutism nourished the passion for domination, land, gold and conquest and resulted in tyranny.

The great revolution of modern times has been the revolution of equality. The idea that all people should be equal in their legal condition has undermined the old structure of authority, hierarchy and deference. The revolution of equality has had two contrary effects on the nature of leadership. For equality, as Alexis de Tocqueville pointed out in his great study *Democracy in America*, might mean equality in servitude as well as equality in freedom.

"I know of only two methods of establishing equality in the political world," Tocqueville wrote. "Rights must be given to every citizen, or none at all to anyone . . . save one, who is the master of all." There was no middle ground "between the sovereignty of all and the absolute power of one man." In his astonishing prediction of 20th-century totalitarian dictatorship, Tocqueville explained how the revolution of equality could lead to the *"Führerprinzip"* and more terrible absolutism than the world had ever known.

But when rights are given to every citizen and the sovereignty of all is established, the problem of leadership takes a new form, becomes more exacting than ever before. It is easy to issue commands and enforce them by the rope and the stake, the concentration camp and the *gulag.* It is much harder to use argument and achievement to overcome opposition and win consent. The Founding Fathers of the United States understood the difficulty. They believed that history had given them the opportunity to decide, as Alexander Hamilton wrote in the first Federalist Paper, whether men are indeed capable of basing government on "reflection and choice, or whether they are forever destined to depend . . . on accident and force."

Government by reflection and choice called for a new style of leadership and a new quality of followership. It required leaders to be responsive to popular concerns, and it required followers to be active and informed participants in the process. Democracy does not eliminate emotion from politics; sometimes it fosters demagoguery; but it is confident that, as the greatest of democratic leaders put it, you cannot fool all of the people all of the time. It measures leadership by results and retires those who overreach or falter or fail.

It is true that in the long run despots are measured by results too. But they can postpone the day of judgment, sometimes indefinitely, and in the meantime they can do infinite harm. It is also true that democracy is no guarantee of virtue and intelligence in government, for the voice of the people is not necessarily the voice of God. But democracy, by assuring the right of opposition, offers built-in resistance to the evils inherent in absolutism. As the theologian Reinhold Niebuhr summed it up, "Man's capacity for justice makes democracy possible, but man's inclination to injustice makes democracy necessary."

A second test for leadership is the end for which power is sought. When leaders have as their goal the supremacy of a master race or the promotion of totalitarian revolution or the acquisition and exploitation of colonies or the protection of greed and privilege or the preservation of personal power, it is likely that their leadership will do little to advance the cause of humanity. When their goal is the abolition of slavery, the liberation of women, the enlargement of opportunity for the poor and powerless, the extension of equal rights to racial minorities, the defense of the freedoms of expression and opposition, it is likely that their leadership will increase the sum of human liberty and welfare.

Leaders have done great harm to the world. They have also conferred great benefits. You will find both sorts in this series. Even "good" leaders must be regarded with a certain wariness. Leaders are not demigods; they put on their trousers one leg after another just like ordinary mortals. No leader is infallible, and every leader needs to be reminded of this at regular intervals. Irreverence irritates leaders but is their salvation. Unquestioning submission corrupts leaders and demands followers. Making a cult of a leader is always a mistake. Fortunately hero worship generates its own antidote. "Every hero," said Emerson, "becomes a bore at last."

The signal benefit the great leaders confer is to embolden the rest of us to live according to our own best selves, to be active, insistent, and resolute in affirming our own sense of things. For great leaders attest to the reality of human freedom against the supposed inevitabilities of history. And they attest to the wisdom and power that may lie within the most unlikely of us, which is why Abraham Lincoln remains the supreme example of great leadership. A great leader, said Emerson, exhibits new possibilities to all humanity. "We feed on genius. . . . Great men exist that there may be greater men."

Great leaders, in short, justify themselves by emancipating and empowering their followers. So humanity struggles to master its destiny, remembering with Alexis de Tocqueville: "It is true that around every man a fatal circle is traced beyond which he cannot pass; but within the wide verge of that circle he is powerful and free; as it is with man, so with communities."

1

A King and His Courage

On the warm, clear evening of August 14, 1760, King Frederick II of Prussia sat with his generals in an army tent, in a rough battle camp near the Silesian town of Liegnitz (now Legnica in southwestern Poland). It had been so hot on that particular summer's day that the tents afforded little comfort to the king and his men. All around his own tent stood those of his weary soldiers, where his troops were eating their rations after the day's long march. At sundown the quiet was disturbed only by the soldiers' low voices and occasional whinnies from their horses, grazing nearby. But this peaceful scene was deceptive, for this was the fourth year of the Seven Years' War, which raged from 1756 to 1763. The night seemed destined to be one of the worst of King Frederick's life.

He was 48 years old, but his haggard appearance made him look much older. Gray-haired, afflicted with bad teeth, severe stomach pains, and gout, he had been so ill all summer that he could not ride his horse. On many occasions during the war, his infirmity forced him to arrive at the scene of battle

In the face of the storm and the threat of shipwreck, I must think, live, and die like a king.
—FREDERICK THE GREAT

When Frederick II ascended the Prussian throne in 1740 he inherited an army of 83,000 men. His father, Frederick William, had ensured Prussia's status as a military power. Frederick made good on his promise to raise Prussia's prestige and has thus been known to history as "Frederick the Great."

THE BETTMANN ARCHIVE

Frederick discovers the body of a soldier who, after being given a handkerchief by the king to bind a head wound, returned to the fighting and was killed. The incident occurred at the Battle of Lobositz in 1756, an early victory for Prussia in the Seven Years' War.

in a carriage. Still, he managed always to clamber atop a horse to observe the fight. His blue coat hung loosely on his thin, bent body but a fierce light still glowed in his pale blue eyes. As he listened to his generals' report, his stern expression showed them that in spite of the bleak prospects, courage still burned in his heart.

The situation was alarming, the generals said. The soldiers were nearly too worn out to fight, and their supply wagons held only enough food for four more days. Meanwhile, huge Austrian and Russian armies were approaching, ready to crush Frederick's smaller force between them. Although the Prussians were gallant fighters, even they knew defeat was nearly certain. Probably many of them would have deserted already, if not for their devotion to King Frederick, whom they called "Old Fritz."

Hearing these reports, Frederick felt terrible discouragement. He had already lost half his army in a disastrous attack on the Russian invaders at Kunersdorf (now Kunowice in western Poland) the previous summer. His new recruits were young, some only 15 years old, and he felt responsible for them. But tomorrow or the next day, he thought, they would probably all die in battle. Then, with Frederick's army defeated, and himself killed or captured, the Russians, French, Austrians, and Swedes would win the war. Only a miracle could save the day, but Frederick feared he had run out of miracles. Still, he would not give up. His resolve could not be broken.

Frederick had not wanted to fight in the first place. He felt he had been forced into the war, which had several causes. In the 18th century much of Europe was not yet divided into the countries we know today. What now approximates modern Germany was then the Holy Roman Empire of the German Nations. This empire was divided into kingdoms, and the Seven Years' War began as a quarrel between Austria and Prussia, having its origin in the earlier War of the Austrian Succession. Soon Austria took France, Russia, and Sweden as allies against Prussia, which had already signed a treaty of alliance with England.

But each of them had its own reason for fighting. Louis XV of France, who always wanted to increase French power and control over the German-speaking nations, disliked Frederick, having heard some rude jokes Frederick had made about him. Besides, France was already fighting England (ruled by King George II) over the colonies in India and America. Thus the English-Prussian treaty made Prussia the enemy of France. Meanwhile, Maria Theresa, queen of Hungary and Bohemia (now Czechoslovakia) and archduchess of Austria, wanted to regain Silesia, which she had ceded to Prussia in an earlier peace treaty. Empress Elizabeth of Russia wanted Poland and feared Prussia would try to keep her from getting it. She also had been the victim of Frederick's witticisms and had developed a dislike for him. For his part, Frederick wanted to hold on to Silesia, and

Louis XV of France assumed the throne when he was only five years old. Reversing his earlier policy, in 1756 he signed the Treaty of Versailles and joined with Austria's ruler, Maria Theresa, against Prussia. The alliance of France, Austria, and Russia left Frederick no alternative but war.

THE BETTMANN ARCHIVE

he wanted to prevent the French from getting the power they desired. Moreover, he doubted the possibility of Austria and France allying against him, as their two royal families, the Habsburgs and the Bourbons, had traditionally been rivals. Sweden was lured into the conflict in the hope of obtaining the Baltic region of Pomerania from Prussia and through payments from the other allies. Finally, since England was fighting France in America (the French and Indian War) and India, it backed Frederick against the French in Europe. In that way, France would have to keep more armies in Europe to fight Frederick, instead of sending them to combat the English for control of the distant and valuable colonial territories.

At first all had gone well for Prussia, and Frederick had won several brilliant victories. But now the English were not sending the kind of help he needed. The huge enemy forces were slowly prevailing, and Prussia's defeat drew near. As he sat sweltering in his tent in the battle camp on that August night in 1760, listening to his generals recite the gloomy facts, Frederick tried to think of a way to save his men. He could not give up, but things looked hopeless.

Suddenly there was a disturbance outside his tent. Through the dusk, by the flickering light of the campfires, Frederick and his generals saw a tattered, staggering figure who had wandered into the camp and was yelling drunkenly that he wanted to talk to the king. Another ruler might have had the rowdy fellow flogged or shot, but Frederick disliked inflicting pain. He would not even use spurs when he rode a horse. As for capital punishment, he was against it except in very serious cases.

Frederick was widely recognized as an intellectual ruler who had associated himself with many of the new philosophical and literary movements then gaining notoriety in Europe. While he was an absolute monarch, he also considered himself the defender of Prussia's *raison d'état* — the interests of state. From the time he had succeeded his father as king on May 31, 1740, however, Frederick was determined to turn Prussia into a leading European

Titles are the decorations of fools; great men need nothing but their names.
—FREDERICK THE GREAT

power. He had rapidly earned a reputation as one of Europe's bravest and most effective soldiers. Nevertheless, despite his warlike qualities, he detested cruelty. His own upbringing had been harsh and painful, which probably helped instill in him a sense of outrage whenever he saw needless cruelty and torment.

At this moment he was also quite desperate to hear any news that might help him find a way out of his dangerous military situation. He ordered the man brought to him and listened to his story. It was a wise decision. The man was an Irishman who had been fighting in the Austrian army but felt he had been treated unjustly. Now he had deserted, and to get revenge he told Frederick that the Austrians were secretly planning to storm the Prussian camp that very night. One force was to seize Frederick's supply wagons, while the other was to slaughter the Prussian soldiers while they slept in their tents.

Frederick realized at once that this deserter had brought salvation. He ordered his soldiers to creep silently away from the encampment. He left peasants and a few of his men to keep the fires burning and make noises, so the Austrians would think the army was still there. Then he and his soldiers went to sleep in a nearby meadow. When the Austrians swept in from the darkness, there was no one in the camp to attack. The Prussians stormed up from behind and engaged them by surprise in a ferocious battle.

A French army of the 18th century marching in formation. France had the mightiest army in Europe and might have defeated the British in the North American colonies and India had Frederick not forced French troops to remain fighting in Europe.

THE BETTMANN ARCHIVE

War in the 1700s required soldiers to march or ride horses 30 or 40 miles a day in all kinds of weather, over all kinds of terrain. Sometimes the soldiers were so tired when they arrived at the battle site that they had to rest before they could begin fighting. Everything they needed was hauled along with them in supply wagons, which had to be defended against enemy raiders. When food or water ran out, they foraged in the countryside, eating whatever they could find. Often they marched for days with barely any rations.

Battle itself was usually at close range. Cavalry soldiers met close up, slashing and stabbing with their sabers while trying to control their lunging horses. Armed with muskets, the infantry struggled on foot to attack the enemy's artillery and put it out of action, all the while trying to avoid being trampled by the cavalry. They fired volleys at their foes from distances seldom greater than 300 paces. Once the artillery's big guns had been fired several times, the battlefield filled with thick, choking smoke from the gunpowder, making it difficult to breathe and almost impossible to see. At times, battles were lost or won simply because the soldiers lost track of their own or their enemies' positions. Screaming men, roaring guns and clashing swords, the horses' huge bodies crashing to earth with men beneath them — that was the type of battle fought in the hours before dawn on that morning in August 1760.

Fighting against Frederick was an Austrian army led by the skillful general Baron Gideon Ernst von Laudon. Further Austrian forces, led by Count Leopold von Daun, stood ready to provide reinforcement some two and a half miles away. It was Daun who had defeated the seemingly unstoppable Frederick at the Battle of Kolin (in Bohemia, now Czechoslovakia) on June 18, 1757, with the Prussians sustaining heavy casualties. The Prussian defeat had brought tears to the eyes of their disappointed king. Frederick had been forced to retreat to the electorate of Saxony. Laudon and the Austrians had been with the Russians at Kunersdorf on August 12, 1759, where, with the Prussians on the brink of victory, the tide of the battle had suddenly turned

Maria Theresa, queen of Bohemia and Hungary, became archduchess of Austria and then empress of the Holy Roman Empire and was a lifelong adversary of Frederick's. He once remarked, "She is always weeping but always annexing."

and half of Frederick's men were slaughtered by the combined Austrian and Russian forces.

Both men were formidable commanders who had more than proved their mettle against Frederick. Now, not sparing himself, Frederick plunged with his men into the thick of combat. At the Battle of Kolin the king had charged the Austrians virtually singlehandedly when his infantry were too tired to follow. This time his horse was shot from under him, his uniform was shredded in the struggle, and the Prussians again sustained heavy losses, but when the fighting was done, 6,000 Austrians had been killed or wounded and 4,000 were prisoners. Daun had been ordered by Queen Maria Theresa, who ruled Austria, to "neglect no opportunity for giving battle." On hearing of Laudon's utter defeat, he abandoned any attempt at rescue, and the Prussians were victorious. They had lost 3,400 of the 16,000 troops engaged in combat.

At midday, Frederick finally marched his dazed and fatigued men through the summer heat, away from the battlefield. Everyone walked, even the ailing king, so that the wounded could ride. When they saw their ruler trudging and sweating through the dust of a parched, blazing August day, Frederick's men realized once again that he was willing to undergo the same dangers and discomforts experienced by the common foot soldier. They knew also that his unusual decision of the night before had saved them. Had Frederick not listened to the deserter, the Austrians' trick would have worked, and they would all have perished.

King George II of England was Frederick's uncle. Though few of his troops fought with Prussia in the Seven Years' War, George was generous in subsidizing Frederick's army. He set up an "army of observation" in the western German states and pinned the French down in a war over the North American colonies.

Frederick's willingness to listen was but one example of his hunger for useful information, however doubtful the source. Frederick was not just a rigid military man who thought only of tactics and discipline but a ruler of keen wit and piercing intelligence. Seven years earlier he had been a close friend of Voltaire, the great French thinker and writer. At home, even though he hated getting up early, Frederick rose at four every morning to read and study. On war campaigns, suffering terribly from stomach pains due to porphyria, a disease he inherited from his royal ancestors, he still took extraordinary care to learn about local conditions. He studied maps and walked around the countryside to discover the land contours, sources of food and water, and the conditions and opinions of the native population. He learned the names of his men and often talked and joked with them.

> *He must always be considered one of the greatest captains and masters of the art of war that ever lived.*
> —London *Annual Register* on Frederick in 1786

All this gave him a tremendous advantage in combat. Knowing the terrain, he could avoid its traps (swamps that could bog down his men) and use its other characteristics for tactical purposes (rivers, for example, whose swift waters could stop enemies from advancing against them). His soldiers, knowing that he cared about them and endured many of the same hardships, fought with great loyalty in return.

Historians disagree about when Frederick came to be called Frederick the Great. It may have been soon after troops of the electorate of Saxony were routed by Prussian grenadiers in December 1745 at the Battle of Kesselsdorf. The claim also is made that not until the long War of the Austrian Succession ended in 1748 was the 36-year-old king hailed as "the Great."

Anyone seeing him would have thought he enjoyed leading armies and ruling a kingdom, but he much preferred quieter pursuits: conversation, gardening, music, and poetry. Only his royal birth forced him into a position of power, and for a while in his youth he had rebelled angrily. Finally, however, he realized that a man who inherits a kingdom must rule and defend it.

Unlike other brilliant soldiers of the era, Frederick had many interests besides military ones. This portrait reveals two of his favorite pastimes: literature and his greyhound dogs. His learning was so great that he was more than once called "the philosopher-king."

While some have said that he won the Battle of Liegnitz through luck, because a deserter happened to find his camp, Frederick's men knew luck only helped those who were prepared to use it as their king had, with knowledge, energy, courage, and common sense. If he had lost this battle, Prussia would almost surely have been swept away. Instead, Frederick led his small nation successfully through the Seven Years' War and afterwards rebuilt Prussia into a force that helped shape modern Europe and the history of the world.

2

Raised to Be King

Frederick Hohenzollern, the third child of Frederick William I, King of Brandenburg-Prussia, and Queen Sophia Dorothea, was born in Berlin on January 24, 1712, and was christened as Karl Frederick. Two previous sons died as infants before Frederick's birth and so Frederick became the heir to the Prussian throne.

His childhood was a rigidly disciplined one. His every action was regulated by schedule. By the age of seven, his father saw to it that he had a governor, a tutor, a music teacher, and numerous personal servants, all of whom administered the routine that Frederick's father had set down as proper for him. Frederick rose, washed, studied, prayed, ate, practiced music, and played according to schedule. In a note to Frederick's servants, the king ordered: "You must accustom [Fritz] to get out of and into his clothes as fast as is *humanly possible.* You will also see that he learns to put on and take off his clothes himself, *without any help from others*, and that he shall be clean and neat and *not so dirty.* Frederick William."

> *God created donkeys, doric columns, and kings to bear the burdens of the world.*
> —FREDERICK THE GREAT

King Frederick William I of Brandenburg-Prussia thrashes a lazy public official. He established a class of efficient public officials for Prussia, laying the foundation for Frederick's future governmental reforms, but his physical, and possibly mental, illness cast a shadow over Frederick's early adult life.

On January 18, 1701, Frederick I, the elector of Brandenburg (as Frederick III) and Frederick's grandfather, was crowned the first "king in Prussia." Holy Roman Emperor Leopold I approved his kingship so as to gain an ally in the War of the Spanish Succession.

He learned mathematics, German, French, economics, political theory, and theology. His tutor, Jacques Egide Duhan de Jandun, a Frenchman, was an important influence on the boy. He and the crown prince became very close. Against Frederick William's wishes, Duhan taught the boy to read Latin. To his father, the study of Latin in order to read classical Roman literature was a waste of time. A mastery of French and German should be sufficient, he thought, for the practical business of the next king of Brandenburg-Prussia. However, reading these classics would later prove important to Frederick's own views on statesmanship. Caesar and Marcus Aurelius, both emperors of the bygone Roman Empire, were also two writers whose works on war and philosophy greatly influenced Frederick as a military leader and scholar. His father felt that if young Frederick had to read these books, he should read them in French translation.

Strangely, Frederick never learned to speak or write German correctly. Later, he admitted that he spoke German "like a coachman." The language he used regularly throughout his life in speech and correspondence was French.

Although the crown prince was forced to pray each day, he never became a religious man. He was drawn briefly to Calvinism, the Christian faith founded by the 16th-century French religious reformer John Calvin. He did not become a Calvinist, but Calvin's doctrine of *predestination* made a lasting impression on Frederick's basic beliefs. According to this idea, an individual's punishment or heavenly reward after death was already determined, regardless of his actions while alive. Frederick also became convinced that human beings were wicked by nature, a notion that sharply conflicted with certain views of the most important thinkers of the period. He nevertheless adopted many of their ideas as his own.

Frederick's mother, Sophia Dorothea, commissioned this portrait of Wilhelmina and Frederick at ages four and two. Until her death in 1758, Wilhelmina was one of Frederick's closest friends. Frederick said they were "two bodies but with one soul."

Frederick's early interest in Calvinism soon gave way to an enduring admiration for the Rationalist philosophers of the Enlightenment, the intellectual movement that originated in England and France and rapidly became widespread throughout Europe. These writers and scholars argued that man, nature, and society were phenomena that could be explained and understood only through reason — the application of mind and analytic thinking. The 18th-century French philosophers Denis Diderot, Jean d'Alembert, Jean-Jacques Rousseau (who later refused to visit Frederick because of the king's military activities), and the Scottish skeptic David Hume were changing European views of the world. These men of learning represented both scientific and political progress, often advocating democratic government and the principle of human equality. Modern science now stands upon many of the advances made by those who contributed to the Enlightenment (*Aufklärung* in German). Their positions also contradicted older, religious-based explanations of the physical universe and man's place in it. The absolute rule of kings was seriously challenged, culminating in the French Revolution (1789-99), which would overturn the backward and increasingly tyrannical French monarchy.

To Frederick William, the very word *reason* was a cause for suspicion. Reason undermined what kings believed was their God-given right to rule over their people. Rational thinking was a threat to a ruler like Frederick William, who was not above roughing up peasants in the street and demanding that they love him.

In addition to Frederick's other studies, his father taught him the rudiments of military leadership, taking the small boy along to army exercises and giving him a regiment of his own to command. Called the Crown Prince Cadets, this regiment was made up of children and held target-shooting contests under young Frederick's direction.

Still, even as a small boy, Frederick had a rebellious streak. This was initially encouraged by his father, whose behavior toward the child was extremely unpredictable. Frederick and his sister

Wilhelmina sometimes deliberately worked their father into a terrible rage, then ran and hid in their mother's room.

Although frequently ill, Frederick William was a robust, stern man who — unlike his heir — was not drawn to intellectual pursuits. He loved hunting, smoking, and military life and could not understand why his son did not love those things, too. Under his reign, Prussia had finally begun to recover from the devastation it had suffered during the last century in the Thirty Years' War, which lasted from 1618 to 1648. Prussia's cities, towns, farmland, peasantry, military, landowners — all had suffered. Frederick William had instituted programs for the recovery of the Prussian economy and devoted much time and money to developing the military. He intended that his son should carry on his work. Although he enjoyed none of his father's "manly" pastimes, Frederick was forced to participate in all of them.

No one, however, could force him to pretend that he reveled in such rough pursuits. Frederick developed ways to demonstrate his contempt for these activities. Forced to hunt, he would vanish into the woods and be found later playing an air on his flute. Aware that his father, his intellectual inferior, abhorred Frederick's admiration for French language and culture, he defiantly refused to clip his hair in the style of Prussian soldiers and combed it in the French style, into long curls. In answer to a letter from his son in September 1728, Frederick William told Frederick that he was a young man with "a wicked, stubborn mind which does not love his father." He wrote of Frederick, "I can not stand an effeminate fellow whose inclinations are not human, who can not ride or shoot . . . [who] curls his hair like a fop and will not have it cut." The king was also scornful of the keen competition among European courts to outshine one another with finery and dazzling glamor. Under his reign members of the Prussian court wore simple military dress and not the extravagant attire customarily worn by royalty. Frederick also wore only military clothing on becoming king. He usually dressed in plain blue

Frederick was a gifted flutist and composer. Throughout his life, music was a refuge from the problems of state and war. He sometimes spent as many as four hours practicing on his flute, and he transformed the Prussian court into a place where concerts were often given and many eminent musicians were welcome.

coats that he wore until they were tattered.

But what was mischief for Frederick was deadly serious for the unstable king, who began to beat, starve, and generally mistreat the boy with such severity that all the royal families of Europe worried about the child. The boy's mother, Sophia Dorothea, fearing her husband's rages and unable to control Frederick, did not restrain the father from abusing his son or the son from provoking his father.

The result was that by the time he reached his mid-teens, Frederick was wild, cynical, rebellious, and quite uncontrollable. He boldly displayed his growing love for all things French, which his father hated. He mocked his father's religious beliefs, won arguments with him, and later behaved arrogantly, displaying an uncaring attitude. This only threw his father into even more violent rages. Frederick, on the other hand, developed an outwardly cold personality. He learned to cover up signs of anger or unhappiness.

His only real confidante during this confused and unhappy period of his life was his elder sister, Wilhelmina. These two were the oldest surviving children — there were 14 born to the family — and although they sometimes quarrelled, their affection and sympathy for one another never diminished. They took the brunt of their father's physical suffering and growing mental instability, possibly caused by the illness known as manic depression. They also suffered from another cause of unhappiness in the Hohenzollern household: their mother's enormous social ambitions for her children.

As a blood relation to English royalty, Sophia Dorothea, who was also called "Olympia," felt herself entitled to much more elegant surroundings and greater comfort than the unfashionable and somewhat stodgy court in Berlin, the Prussian capital, had to offer. Frederick William had married her because he loved her, but she looked down on the House of Brandenburg and the Hohenzollern family. She felt herself superior to them. As a result, she wanted her children to have those things that she thought had been denied her through her marriage to the Prussian king: luxury, greater power, and fashion. These could best be achieved, she thought, through a marriage alliance with the English royal family.

Sophia Dorothea was from the northern German region then known as the electorate of Hanover. The Hanoverian dynasty proudly basked in the prestige of having already provided one English monarch, Sophia's father, the elector of Hanover, George I. Her brother succeeded him as king of England in 1727, as George II. They are often referred to as the Hanoverian kings.

Electorates were so called because their leaders, the electors, made up the College of Electors, which supposedly elected the emperor of the Holy Roman Empire. This political system, established in A.D. 800, was intended to rule over the German-speaking Catholic lands. For the previous 300 years, however, this empire had been headed by the House of Habsburg. Over the centuries the empire's power had become largely symbolic. With little organizational strength, its existence was threatened by Europe's

> *I herewith beg humbly for forgiveness, and I hope that my dear Papa will forget the fearful hate which appears so clearly in his whole behavior and to which I find it hard to accustom myself.*
> —FREDERICK
> age 16, in a letter to his father

Frederick William regularly held "tobacco parliament" sessions. These were prolonged drinking and smoking bouts with which the king entertained his cronies. The young Frederick regarded these gatherings with contempt but was forced to attend them anyway.

division into Catholic and Protestant nations. Prussia was among the Protestant states, and during Frederick's reign as Prussian king the crumbling Holy Roman system would be toppled by the wars he would fight over Silesia. Meanwhile, the House of Bourbon, which ruled France, regarded the empire as a valued prize, since it encompassed the entire bloc of German states.

During the 1700s the Hanoverians were associated with a group known as the Guelphs. Originally a German political faction that supported the Roman Catholic pope, the Guelphs derived their name from that of the 11th-century duke of Bavaria. In the 12th century they comprised the forces of the dukes of Bavaria and Saxony against the party representing the lords of Hohenstaufen. In Italy the

conflict became a struggle between the Guelphs, on the side of the church, and the Ghibellines, on the side of the various emperors. By Frederick's time, the Guelphs no longer were an actual party linked to the pope. The name referred to those, such as Sophia Dorothea, who had close ties to England and were among Brandenburg's Dutch rivals. English writer and historian Edith Simon sums up the conflict in the Prussian royal household: "The prevailing trend in the King's party was towards Austria; the Queen was for England." An English-Hanoverian faction began to conspire to outmaneuver the pro-Austrian Prussian court. Sophia Dorothea even dreamed of eventually becoming the queen of England. The king was alert to this problem but exaggerated its seriousness.

THE BETTMANN ARCHIVE

Frederick William was frequently subject to uncontrollable temper tantrums. Wilhelmina and Frederick sometimes went without dinner if they provoked the king. Enraged by the crown prince's unusual behavior, Frederick William once nearly strangled his son to death with a curtain cord.

In line with her sentiments, Sophia Dorothea tried to arrange marriages between Wilhelmina and the prince of Wales and between Frederick and Princess Amelia of England. Frederick William opposed the idea, particularly for Frederick, whose rebelliousness caused his father to think him a traitor to the Prussian crown.

When the king put his foot down and stopped the plans for Frederick to wed the English princess, Frederick was thrown into despair. But at the age of 16, he was permitted to visit Dresden, in Saxony, with his father. The visit in 1728 to the fashionable

Dresden court made a considerable impression on the crown prince, further convincing him that life could be so much better if he could somehow manage to escape Berlin and his father's iron discipline. On one occasion his despotic father ordered more than 3,000 of the crown prince's books destroyed. Frederick began to confide in Count Friedrich von Rothenburg, a Prussian ambassador to the French court, and admitted to him that he was planning an escape to Paris. The diplomat urged him not to act rashly, for if the crown prince of Prussia were to run away to France, it would be a very great embarrassment to Prussia. It could even mean war.

So Frederick was compelled to remain at his father's palace in Berlin, where conditions grew worse by the day. When the king was away, life was tolerable. Frederick read, studied, rode his horse, and played the flute with Wilhelmina. But when Frederick William returned home from his trips around the country, suffering from gout and maddening pain from porphyria, Frederick was beaten, starved, and had his hair pulled; he was cruelly mocked and insulted and told that he was a coward for enduring such treatment. At least once the king came very close to murdering his son by strangling him with a curtain cord. If his own father had treated him that way, Frederick William told the youthful prince, "I would have put a bullet through my head; but you have not got it in you even to do that." It was perhaps this statement that put a very dangerous idea into young Frederick's mind.

All right, Frederick must have thought, I will not kill myself, that is for certain, but I will run away — and without help from ambassadors. I have my friends, and they will help me. I will go to France all on my own.

He was determined to escape, and he nearly succeeded. But he had underestimated his father's even more serious determination to keep him. Nor could he imagine the severity of the punishment he and others would suffer for the attempt. The dangerous plot not only failed but resulted in punishments so terrible that Frederick's entire view of life was changed.

When Frederick was 18 years old, it was decided that he should accompany his father on a trip around Germany. Part of the journey would bring the party near the French frontier. His two best friends, Lieutenants Peter Karl Christoph von Keith and Hans Hermann von Katte, collected money, maps, and clothes to be secretly delivered to Frederick while he was still with his father. With their help, Frederick thought, he would flee across the border and not reappear until he was in France. He thought that he might go to Holland from there. He would then be out of his father's reach.

Unfortunately, some letters detailing the secret project were delivered not to Frederick's friend Katte but to Katte's cousin, a cavalry captain with the same last name. The captain read the letters, then

Frederick Louis, prince of Wales, was the son of George II. Frederick William's Hanoverian wife, Queen Sophia Dorothea, wanted Wilhelmina to marry him and Frederick to marry the prince's sister Amelia, thus solidifying Prussia's ties with Great Britain.

sent them to Colonel Friedrich Wilhelm von Rochow, who was traveling with Frederick and knew that Frederick might try to run away.

Thus, at Frankfurt, Frederick was delivered into his father's furious presence. After a scene during which the king was barely restrained from killing his son, Frederick was imprisoned under guard but was able to warn his friend Keith, who ran away. Katte's seizure was also ordered, but instead of fleeing, as his merciful commanding officer had given him time to do, Frederick's unthinking friend loitered around until the officer could do nothing except arrest him.

At the military tribunal that followed, Katte was sentenced to life imprisonment. Frederick's case was submitted to the same court. He was charged with desertion, which would carry the death penalty if he were convicted. The members of the tribunal did not want to pass judgment on the crown prince. After all, if they found him innocent, they might offend the king, Frederick William, who would surely make them feel his wrath. If they found Frederick guilty and sentenced him to death, he might escape his sentence. Then, when Frederick became king himself, he would remember the tribunal members and what they had nearly done to him. Who could tell if he would take revenge on them?

To avoid this possibility, the tribunal returned Frederick's case to the king, saying they were unable to decide the matter because Frederick was of royal birth. Frederick William took the whole matter into his own hands, starting with the case of Frederick's friend Katte. He changed Katte's sentence from life imprisonment to death. Frederick was placed in a prison at Küstrin. On the morning of November 6, 1730, Katte was led into the courtyard outside the prison, where Frederick could see him from an upper window. There, after the youths exchanged a few words, with Frederick begging his friend's forgiveness and Katte replying that there was nothing to forgive, Hans Hermann von Katte was beheaded with a sword.

Frederick was obliged to watch the dreadful execution of his dearest friend. It was from this day on

After witnessing the execution of his close friend Hans von Katte, Frederick slowly came to terms with his irascible father. Locked up in the prison-fortress at Küstrin, he grew to manhood and realized that his responsibilities to the state outweighed his own feelings.

that Frederick changed his behavior, his attitude, and the entire conduct of his life. Two weeks later, Frederick left the prison at Küstrin for a house in the town. Although he was to serve an unspecified term in the Küstrin administration and still lived under very strict regulation — his social life, especially, was restricted — it was better than prison and certainly better than being executed himself, which was what he had expected.

The director of the town chamber of Küstrin, or local government, taught Frederick about town government and also instructed the crown prince in the history, geography, and economy of Prussia and the other German principalities. For his part, Frederick learned from the director, mostly because in the boring town of Küstrin there was little else to do but read, study, think — and examine his conscience.

He must have felt deeply saddened and guilty about the death of his friend Katte. After all, the plot to escape was all Frederick's idea, but clever, charming Katte had lost his life for it. Imprisoned, Frederick was left to contemplate his own responsibility for the bloodshed and grief that came out of this youthful escapade. He was forced to conclude that the fault had been his own; he had failed to think about what might happen to others — only about what he wanted for himself. As he remembered with remorse again and again the terrible moment when Katte died, he began to learn a hard lesson about responsibility.

Frederick deeply mourned Katte's death, but from this tragic and terrifying experience the young crown prince better understood the use and abuse of power. He had possessed it, and used it irresponsibly in persuading his friends to help with a childish plot. He had witnessed his father use the same power, on the morning when the executioner's sword severed Katte's neck in the Küstrin prison courtyard. But he knew power could also be used wisely and fairly. During his lonely stay at Küstrin, he contemplated these matters. By the end of the ordeal he was no longer merely a rebellious boy. He would somehow turn this disaster to some practical use by learning from it whatever would help his future plans for Brandenburg-Prussia.

Meanwhile the old king vowed that Frederick would languish at Küstrin until his change of heart was complete, "and I," said the king, "will know when that has happened." While still toying with Frederick's fate, the king remarked coolly to his war minister, Friedrich Wilhelm von Grumbkow, "I hope he won't end on the gallows yet, though I doubt it myself." In August 1731 his father came to visit him at Küstrin. More than once, Frederick fell to his knees before his father. He confessed that he had wanted to run away to England. After the king explained how merciful he had been to his family despite their scandalous behavior (the king suspected that Frederick had ultimately planned to reach England and that Sophia Dorothea and Wilhelmina had been involved in the plot), he spoke in reassuring tones to his son. He then got into his carriage and drove away.

In November that same year Wilhelmina was wedded to a more appropriate suitor, Prince Frederick of Bayreuth. Realizing that he could appear outwardly cooperative while continuing to think as he wished, he sent some scathing verses to Grumbkow, who had tried to gain Frederick's trust by posing as the crown prince's confidant. In them, Frederick explained his new outlook:

> When your household overseers
> Behave themselves like buccaneers,
> Simply do as you are bidden—
> Think your thoughts, but keep them hidden.

In November Frederick was allowed to return to Berlin.

From then on he gave up any outward show of rebellion. Rather than continue a losing battle against his father's expectations, he decided to play the part the king demanded. Probably Frederick drew from his own experience when he wrote, "Learn to appear artfully what you are not." Within a very few years his resolution was put to several dangerous and difficult tests, ordeals for which he needed all his strength simply to survive. In 1731 Frederick gained the mind of a king.

Good fortune is often more disastrous for princes than adversity. The former intoxicates, but the latter makes them careful and modest.
—FREDERICK THE GREAT

3

The Young Philosopher-King

On June 12, 1733, Frederick bowed once again to his father's wishes and married Princess Elizabeth Christina of Brunswick-Bevern, a relative of the Austrian emperor, Charles VI. He did not love her. In fact, she was chosen for him by Grumbkow, and the engagement was announced long before he even met her. In the 18th century Europe's royal houses prearranged the marriages of their young people for political and social reasons. Certainly, few royal marriages could have been more politically motivated than young Frederick's. In addition to thinking that marriage would be good for his son, Frederick William was persuaded by the arguments of his minister Grumbkow and Count Ludwig Heinrich von Seckendorf, the Austrian ambassador. Having urged the king to prevent Frederick from marrying an English princess, they wanted to block any further English influence on the Prussian court. Another reason for arranging Frederick's marriage was to keep Prussia subordinate to the Habsburg rulers in Austria. At this time the Habsburgs also controlled Silesia, Bohemia, Hungary,

> *Rulers must possess ambition, but this ambition must be wise, moderate, and enlightened by reason.*
> —FREDERICK THE GREAT

The famed composer Johann Sebastian Bach, visiting Sans Souci in 1747, improvises at the harpsichord while Frederick listens. *The Musical Offering*, **dedicated to Frederick and based on a theme the king supplied, was Bach's famous souvenir of their meeting.**

The young Frederick accompanied the great general Prince Eugene of Savoy (shown here) on his unsuccessful campaign against the French in 1734. Eugene predicted that Prussia's neighbors would be surprised by Frederick's aggressive policies once he ascended the throne.

the Austrian or southern Netherlands (now Belgium), North Serbia (now in Yugoslavia), Wallachia (now part of Romania), as well as parts of Italy and Germany. Moreover, Grumbkow had his own hidden ties with the Habsburgs, which England had tried to reveal so as to endanger his position with the Prussian king. The plot did not succeed, and Frederick William resolved that the crown prince would marry according to Seckendorf and Grumbkow's plan. Frederick gave in to his father's wishes but then begged Grumbkow to change the king's mind, "for the sake of Christ's wounds."

After mastering the politics and intrigues of palace life, the young participants in such arranged marriages sometimes had few personal allies. Determined to make the best of the circumstances in which they found themselves, they often grew intensely devoted to one another.

But love was not necessarily a vital requirement in a royal household, even in a marriage. Although he always treated Elizabeth with respect, Frederick did not attempt to become close to her. At one point, seeing how little attention Frederick paid to his fiancée, Frederick William furiously demanded that the crown prince write letters to her at once. Frederick remarked, "The idea is to beat love into me with a stick. . . . What am I to write her?" He would marry her, he said, to please his father, but then he would do as he wished. Indeed, that was what he did.

Although he said later that he had fulfilled his marital duty by having conjugal relations with Elizabeth, the couple did not have any children. Some say a childhood injury or illness made Frederick unable to sire children, but no definite explanation has been found for his not producing an heir. There also was no obvious reason for Frederick's indifference toward Elizabeth, a lack of interest he made almost no effort to hide. Elizabeth, for her part, seems to have possessed considerable strength of character, for she behaved throughout her life with perfect dignity and correctness despite Frederick's coldness and neglectful treatment of her. In 1732, when Frederick agreed to become engaged to the princess from the House of Brunswick, he won freedom from his father's tyrannical household at Küstrin — a place where he was treated, he thought, no better than a galley slave. He took up residence at Neuruppin, a nearby garrison town. There he served as a colonel in charge of an army regiment. Although closely scrutinized by the king, Frederick became increasingly absorbed in his new military interests and responsibilities. Meanwhile, Elizabeth was isolated from her husband's newfound military life. She resided in a château called Schönhausen, a present from Frederick William.

The pattern for the couple's nearly lifelong separation was established in 1734, soon after their marriage. That year Frederick went on an expedition with 10,000 of his father's soldiers to defend the neighboring kingdom of Austria against the French, who were attacking along the Rhine. It was an exciting journey for the 22-year-old Frederick, who had looked forward to fighting one day under the famous general Prince Eugene of Savoy. In this, however, he was disappointed. The French general Count Maurice de Saxe prevented Eugene's forces from getting near enough to help hold Philippsburg or to participate in any of the fighting at all. But the trip did offer other rewards.

Besides escaping the company of Elizabeth, he got to travel, which he had not done since before the death of Hans Katte. He met new friends, whom he greatly enjoyed, and who would prove helpful to him. Most important of all he learned that the Austrian army was weaker and commanded by less effective officers than he had been led to expect. If the Austrians had known what use Frederick would later make of this information, they might not have let him observe their armed forces so closely. The desire to take the reins of royal authority had been stimulated. Frederick now felt driven to become a general who would achieve great victories for his future kingdom.

Frederick is the soloist in a concert at Sans Souci ("Without Cares"), the palace he built at Potsdam. His teacher, the composer Johann Joachim Quantz, was associated with the Prussian court for 30 years and wrote the highly regarded *Essay on a Method for Playing the Transverse Flute.*

fiane par Boulenveh

Count Maurice de Saxe commanded the French army that defeated Prince Eugene and the Austrians at Philippsburg in 1734. In the War of the Austrian Succession and the two Silesian wars he was Frederick's ally against the Austrian ruler, Maria Theresa.

For the time being, however, Frederick filed the knowledge away in his mind. Returning home, he found his father very ill, and he began to think that soon he would be king. But the old man recovered yet again, and at this Frederick must have felt a mixture of relief and disappointment. Only when the throne became his would Frederick finally escape his father's tyranny. Only then would he be able to put into practice his own ideas for ruling Prussia. Frederick must also have dreaded his father's approaching end. Now that Frederick was grown, the two men understood each other better and had worked out ways of getting along. However strained and difficult their relationship had been — and still was at times — they were after all father and son, and the bond was a powerfully emotional one for them both.

But with no wars to fight and no prospect of assuming the throne any time very soon, there was little for Frederick to do but go to Rheinsberg, where Frederick William had bought property for the prince and princess and where an enormous, lovely castle had been rebuilt for them. There Frederick read and studied, laying the groundwork for one of his subsequent nicknames: the philosopher-king. He also practiced the flute, an instrument he had loved since childhood and for which he wrote more than 100 sonatas and concertos. For many years he used the instrument as a form of recreation and meditation; he began playing soon after rising in the morning as his mind poured over the day's business.

His interest in music was a lifelong passion that produced enduring results. His flute teacher, Johann Joachim Quantz, spent more than 30 years with Frederick, and during that time Quantz wrote some 300 compositions for the instrument. He also wrote a book entitled *Essay on a Method for Playing the Transverse Flute*, still a respected work on the subject. Later, as king, Frederick employed in his court many other prominent musicians of his day. Johann Sebastian Bach's third son, Carl Philipp Emanuel Bach, also a composer, was Frederick's harpsichordist. Carl Friedrich Christian Fasch, another of Frederick's accompanists, was a composer and teacher of composers. Fasch was well known to Ludwig van Beethoven and was founder of the cho-

Frederick with his retinue on the lake at Rheinsberg in 1739, the year before succeeding his father as king. In addition to his musical interests and extensive reading, Frederick was an avid writer of verse. His intellectual pursuits angered Frederick William.

ral organization that later became the *Berliner Sing-akademie*. Carl Heinrich Graun, musical director of Frederick's court in Potsdam, outside Berlin, wrote more than 30 operas. His brother Johann Gottlieb Graun, in Berlin, composed 100 symphonies, 20 violin concertos, and many other works.

In 1747 Johann Sebastian Bach composed *The Musical Offering*, a group of pieces, including two fugues, canons, and later a sonata, on a theme suggested by Frederick; the first letters of the inscription read *Regis Iussu Cantio Et Reliqua Canonica Arte Resoluta* — A Theme and Other Things Worked Out In Canon By the King's Command.

The evenings at Rheinsberg were extremely lively. The household put on musical performances, plays, poetry readings, and other entertainments in which everyone participated either as performers or as audience. Parties of distinguished visitors came to Rheinsberg to enjoy Frederick's company and hospitality, for the young prince was a charming, witty host. The atmosphere in his palace was cultivated and the conversation always sparkling and well informed.

There, also, Frederick wrote letters — hundreds and hundreds of letters, for getting and sending mail was one of his greatest enjoyments. After he began writing to Voltaire, the great French man of letters, the two corresponded for the rest of Voltaire's life. Frederick exchanged letters also with his friends and relatives, especially his beloved sister Wilhelmina, and with anyone else who would correspond on matters of interest to him.

That requirement was easily fulfilled, for Frederick's interests were far-ranging. He cared about politics and military matters, of course, for he knew they would someday be crucially important to him. But he was deeply involved not only in music but also in poetry, philosophy, history, and economic thought, as well as more mundane matters such as gardening and the proper care of dogs and horses. His wide-ranging curiosity would serve him well later, when he became king, and so would his habit of inquiring into almost any topic that presented itself.

The Bettmann Archive

A sample of Frederick's handwriting. A prodigious letter writer, he was also the author of several works on politics, such as *Forms of Government and Duties of Princes* and *The History of My Own Times*.

But Frederick's broad interests and his steady letter-writing also enlivened his own existence. During the 1700s letters were an immensely important form of communication, and luckily the letters and diaries left by Frederick reveal much about his life and times.

At Rheinsberg, Frederick also began his career as a serious student of politics, warfare, and history. He corresponded with the Saxon statesmen Ulrich Friedrich von Suhm and Count Ernst Christoph Manteuffel, both among the finest minds in Europe at the time. But his days of peaceful study and happy leisure could not last forever, and after several of the calmest, most pleasant years of Frederick's life, two events turned his existence upside-down.

First, he became seriously ill with the disease that had afflicted Frederick William for so long and often drove the old man into rages of agony. Now Frederick realized why his father had been unpredictable, difficult, even cruel, for he began to suffer the same awful miseries himself. Medicine has only now begun to understand the causes of porphyria, the inherited disease that is believed to have caused Frederick and his father so much pain and difficulty. Though it remains incurable, in the 18th century there was no effective treatment even for the pain, and Frederick could do little but suffer until the attacks passed.

Frederick stands beside the open coffin of his great-grandfather Frederick William, "the Great Elector." The founder of Brandenburg-Prussia, he was the first to build up the Prussian military. As king, Frederick would carry on and strengthen the military tradition in Prussia.

Frederick William inspects the Grenadier Guards, his private regiment of giant soldiers. His eccentric preoccupation with this unit of gigantic men was the talk of European courts. He even kidnaped unusually tall foreigners to serve in the regiment. On becoming king, Frederick had the guards disbanded.

No sooner had he recovered his health than Frederick William's health took a serious turn for the worse. He had been ill for so long, it must have seemed to Frederick that his father might go on that way indefinitely — sinking into misery and then recovering, over and over again. But it was not to be; at the age of 52, the older man could not withstand any more attacks.

Thus, one day in the spring of 1740, Frederick was called to his father's side. After years of alternating resentment and forgiveness on both sides, the two men were finally reconciled. The now enfeebled king made arrangements for his funeral and gave Frederick a few last-minute pieces of advice. On May 31, 1740, Frederick William died. At once

Frederick's life as a gentleman-scholar was transformed into that of a responsible young monarch. All the years of writing and studying gave way to action, to a life devoted to governing and war. When the old king died, the last hints of Frederick's boyhood disappeared. At the age of 28, Frederick was king of Prussia.

Frederick William had badly wanted to regain certain territories for the glory of Brandenburg-Prussia. The region of Pomerania had already been conquered by the elector of Brandenburg, Frederick William (Frederick's great-grandfather); the duchies of Jülich and Berg on the Rhine River were eventually obtained from Austria through sacrificing a treaty with England and France. But "the Soldier-King," as the cantankerous Frederick William was called, had not gained Silesia, the Austrian-controlled area to the south of Brandenburg-Prussia, along the Oder River, in what is now largely southwest Poland. Frederick William had long contended that Silesia belonged to Prussia, but he had not seen his dream realized. Though he built up his military forces, he hesitated to use them and warned against taking part in what he called "unjust wars." Stability in foreign affairs, it seemed, had been his greatest concern. To protect that stability, the old king had signed 40 agreements. To Frederick, the agreements were a long list of embarrassments.

Now Frederick, once the bookish poet and musician, wanted to go to war to settle this claim to Silesia once and for all. He possessed a substantial legacy from his father: an army of 83,000 soldiers, including the famed Grenadier Guards (the "Longfellows"), made up of unusually tall soldiers who had been handpicked by Frederick William. Frederick did away with this unit, which had been an obsession for his father, and proceeded to raise 16 infantry battalions in its place. He also had at his disposal some 8 million *talers* (the currency used in Prussia) as well as a developing industrial economy. "I wish," he wrote, "for the Prussian state to raise herself out of the dust . . . to bring the Protestant faith to flower in Europe and the Empire, to become the refuge of the oppressed . . . and the terror of the unjust."

For every state, from the smallest to the largest, the principle of enlargement is the fundamental law of life.
—FREDERICK THE GREAT

4

Rendezvous with Glory

In the summer of 1740, without much ceremony or fanfare, Frederick swore to be a good king to Prussia and set about fulfilling his oath and his destiny. Under his father's rule Prussian subjects had been tortured as a means of getting them to confess to crimes. Their newspapers were censored, and certain religious beliefs and practices were prohibited. Grain prices were apt to fluctuate, based on good or poor harvests, affecting both farmers and consumers. Also, the Berlin Academy had fallen into neglect after many of its intellectuals were exiled.

One such scholar was the philosopher Christian von Wolff. Frederick often showed indifference toward German thought and literature. However, in his first letter to Voltaire in 1736 (whom he met four years later), he praised Wolff's gigantic *Rational Ideas on God, the World, the Soul of Man, and on All Things in General.* Angered by Wolff's argument that man was predestined to be served by a universe created for his benefit, Frederick William made him leave Prussia in 1723. Having lauded Wolff's ideas because they followed "each other geometrically and are connected . . . like the links of a chain," Frederick restored the thinker to his former professorship at the University of Halle.

The true religion of a prince is his interest and his glory.
—FREDERICK THE GREAT

Frederick resettles immigrants from Salzburg, Austria, in Prussia. These immigrants were to establish weaving as a major Prussian industry. Frederick was to prove himself an enlightened ruler who reformed Prussia's agriculture, legal system, industry, and government.

Charles VI was elected emperor of the Holy Roman Empire of the German Nations in 1711. The empire, which Frederick called simply "the system," was by the 18th century essentially a relic of the past. Through the Pragmatic Sanction of 1724, Charles declared his daughter, Maria Theresa, his heir as ruler of the empire.

During the first few days of Frederick's reign, he ended censorship and the torture of civilians in his kingdom, and set reasonable prices on grain so that neither farmers nor the people would go hungry during the poor harvest that was expected that year. Much to the surprise of many observers, he did not set up his friends in high-paying jobs without regard to their abilities. Instead he retained most of his father's advisers and ministers, brought back teachers and officials whom his father had exiled, and put all of them into posts that were suited to their knowledge and experience. He also employed his friends, but before he did so he made sure they had talent, and once they were on the job he required them to work hard. Once he had arranged Prussia's internal affairs to at least his temporary satisfaction — it took him only about a week, working 20 hours a day — he turned his attention to neighboring kingdoms.

The new king's army had been expertly trained and organized by the brilliant soldier Prince Leopold Maximilian von Anhalt-Dessau, or the "Old Dessauer," as he was called. He was the commander and strategist who taught the Prussian soldiers the ancient Roman technique of marching in cadence and drilled them in maneuvers until they were a marvel of mobility. A force consisting of tens of thousands of men could, by Anhalt-Dessau's methods, be moved about a field of battle much more swiftly and accurately than the enemy's army, thus outmaneuvering its foe even when it was outnumbered. The Old Dessauer put into use the iron ramrod, replacing the old wooden rods previously used to pack gunpowder and wadding into the guns. This strengthened the Prussian artillery by making it possible to fire the guns much more rapidly. The following December, Anhalt-Dessau and the revitalized Prussian army invaded Silesia.

Frederick was resolute about using these methods and resources. This was easier than it might otherwise have been because German politics were in considerable confusion. The House of Habsburg, which ruled Austria, was thrown into a crisis when Emperor Charles VI died on October 20, 1740. Without any male heirs, the Habsburgs were to be ruled by Charles's daughter, Maria Theresa. By declaring the Pragmatic Sanction in 1724 and obtaining its approval throughout Europe, Charles thought he had made certain that the Habsburg's empire would be transferred to Maria Theresa. As a result, she would head the Holy Roman Empire. In the meantime, no one really thought much of Frederick or imagined he could be dangerous. All that most European, and even German, rulers knew of the young Prussian king was that he liked to read and play music and had failed in his youth to escape Frederick William's clutches. They thought of him as a weak, somewhat foolish fellow, who certainly would never have the nerve to attack them. Frederick, however, thought the confusion engendered by Maria Theresa's succession provided a golden opportunity to obtain Silesia.

Frederick called his minister Count Heinrich von

Podewils and Major-General Count Kurt Christoph von Schwerin at once to inform them of his plans. He instructed Podewils to set to work at once on finding a justification for invading Silesia. Both were shocked by Frederick's refusal to accept anything but a military solution. Did not the young king understand that Prussia was not strong enough to risk war? Frederick brushed these fears aside. Since Prussia had no legal basis for going to war at this time, one needed to be invented. Podewils obeyed his king and contrived a legal justification for invading Silesia. When he received the document, Frederick was so pleased with this bit of handiwork that he wrote in its margin, "Bravo: the work of an excellent charlatan!" Seven weeks later, having met with almost no resistance at all, he took possession of the rich land. Maria Theresa was furious, but there was little she could do, at least on the diplomatic front. Public opinion all over Europe was on her side, but when Frederick later moved armies into the principal cities of Silesia, no country would send troops to help her. That turned out to be lucky for Frederick, for invading Silesia was one thing, but keeping the conquered land was another. Only the excellent generals his father had left him kept Frederick's initial conquest from turning into a bloodbath. At the Battle of Mollwitz in April 1741, his lack of battlefield experience was most painfully demonstrated to him: things went badly almost from the start, and Frederick, to avoid capture, galloped away from the fighting.

But while he fled, Anhalt-Dessau, one of the most brilliant military leaders of his day, and Schwerin, also a formidable commander, rescued the situation for the Prussians. Schwerin more than proved his worth at Mollwitz. Frederick's forces were numerically equal to the Austrians. He had three times as many field guns as they had, but his cavalry was driven into disarray by the Austrian field marshal Count Wilhelm von Neipperg. When the Austrians tried to press their advantage by attacking the infantry, however, Schwerin ingeniously directed his men to draw back and form an angled line. Thus

the infantry took a most advantageous firing position that could not be broken by the charging Austrians. Dessau's iron ramrod turned out to be invaluable, as it allowed the infantry to shoot twice as fast as the Austrians. The Austrians attacked the Prussian line five times, and five times the Prussian guns drove them off. At last Neipperg backed away into the night. Having ridden away from the first battle of his kingship, Frederick did not learn of his victory until 10 hours later.

Frederick struggled with thoughts of death the night before the Battle of Mollwitz in April 1741, during the First Silesian War. After the inexperienced young ruler fled the scene, the Prussians were led to victory by Count Kurt Christoph von Schwerin, later killed in the Seven Years' War.

Maria Theresa was getting ready to go to Pressburg (now Bratislava), then the capital of Hungary, for her coronation as the queen of Hungary. The House of Habsburg had held the right to succession to the Hungarian throne since 1526. Meanwhile, on June 4, 1741, Prussia agreed to a defensive alliance with France. In addition, the French rejected the Pragmatic Sanction and named Elector Charles Albert of Bavaria as their candidate for emperor of the Holy Roman Empire. Already shocked by this sudden turn of events, Maria Theresa was stunned to see the French mobilize their army and join forces with the Bavarians. Some 40,000 Bavarian and French troops were on the move toward Austria and Hanover. By September Maria Theresa was beseeching the Hungarian aristocracy to take arms against invaders of her realm.

Niccolò Machiavelli, the Italian Renaissance statesman and political theorist, is best known for his book *The Prince*. Though in his book *Anti-Machiavel* Frederick condemned Machiavelli's theories, his military and diplomatic policies reflected Machiavelli's influence.

In the meantime, Frederick had the upper hand in his dealings with France and Maria Theresa. He was prepared to disavow his treaty with France if in doing so he could obtain greater satisfaction from Austria. While the French were temporarily his allies, Frederick realized that in the long run they presented a more significant threat to him than did Austria. His quarrel with Maria Theresa was essentially over the possession of Silesia, but France had designs on all of Germany. Here Frederick demonstrated one of his more controversial theories of leadership: he believed that a king must be willing to sacrifice even his own word of honor to protect his people. For, as he once stated, "It is better that the sovereign should break his word than that the people should perish." One critical eyewitness to Frederick's willingness to break treaties noted: "Upon all occasions he declares his disregard of treaties and guarantees . . . when he is in a condition to break them to his advantage."

Frederick's thoughts in this regard did not seem so very different from those of Niccolò Machiavelli, the 15th-century Italian Renaissance statesman and writer whose works on history and government Frederick had studied. Frederick wrote an attack on Machiavelli's most famous work, *The Prince*, which first appeared in 1513. Entitled *Anti-Machiavel*, the work was Frederick's first published writing as king. (Frederick's first book, written in 1738, was *Reflections on the Political Condition of Europe*.) Completed in 1739, *Anti-Machiavel* was intended as a direct criticism of *The Prince*, which was thought by many to be cynical and even immoral. Nevertheless, it is noted time and again that Frederick's deeds often reflected the policies and conduct that Machiavelli described in his book. One of its most important principles was that rulers ought to put the state's welfare above all else — which Frederick did. Indeed, Frederick saw himself as "first servant of the State." Unlike the great king of France Louis XIV, however, who died three years after Frederick's birth and who fought to expand French territorial control, Frederick did not believe in the divine right of kings. While Louis did all that he

> *A prince must know how to play the beast as well as the man.*
> —NICCOLÒ MACHIAVELLI
> Italian political philosopher

The Arte of warre,
written first in Italia
by Nicholas Machiauell, and set
forthe in Englishe by Peter
Whitehorne, studient at Graies Inne:
with an addicio of other like Mar-
tialle feates and experimen-
tes, as in a Table in the
ende of the Booke
maie appere.

Anno. M.D.LX.
Menß.Iulij.

The title page of an early English language edition of Machiavelli's *The Arte of Warre* dating from 1560. Frederick's own considerable writings on warfare include *Instructions for his Generals* and *Military Testaments*.

could to make himself the center of power, and even declared that the state and himself were one and the same, Frederick ruled, he claimed, to serve the state. In 1777, after reigning for 37 years, he explained in his book *Forms of Government and Duties of Princes*, "We should have to be insane to imagine that men once said to one of their kind: we shall raise you above us because we like to be slaves. . . . On the contrary, men said: we need you, to insure that the laws by which we wish to be governed will be maintained, and that we will be wisely ruled and defended. . . . We demand that you respect our freedom."

Although his *Anti-Machiavel* was inspired by the possibility of a good, just, and kind ruler, rather than Machiavelli's cruel and ruthless ones, Frederick believed that a state must accomplish three things: preserve itself and increase its power, make only alliances that are favorable to itself, and be "respected and feared in the most difficult times." In Frederick's opinion the Italian princes Machiavelli used as examples were "a breed of mongrels."

Frederick's diplomatic maneuvering was intended to secure Silesia in the shortest possible time and at the lowest cost. His finances were far from lavish. As German historian Gerhard Ritter explains, "What he needed were quick, sharp blows and rapid decisions."

Unbeknownst to his French allies, Frederick went to bargain with Maria Theresa. If she promised not to put up resistance over his claim to Silesia, he told her, he would betray the French and renounce the treaty he had signed with them in June 1741.

With reluctance, but also with relief, Maria Theresa's military forces secretly agreed with Frederick on October 9, 1741, to a ceasefire. After the Convention of Klein-Schnellendorf, as this agreement was called, Frederick's war against Austria — or his war *for* Silesia — was fought for him by the French and Bavarians. Franco-Bavarian armies crossed the Austrian frontier on October 24, only weeks after his secret talks with the Austrians. By late November Bavarian troops had defeated the Austrian defenders of Prague in Bohemia (now Czechoslovakia). Field Marshal Neipperg's forces were allowed to withdraw from Silesia without suffering any further defeats. When they learned that Frederick had deceived them by making a separate peace with the Austrians, the French were horrified. The result was that the French were trapped in Prague and under attack by the Austrians without any hope that the Prussians would help them escape. Five months later, with Prague running short of food, 14,000 French soldiers were allowed to take supplies sufficient for 12 days and go on a "foraging expedition"; they were also allowed to take their guns in case there were Austrian soldiers in the vicinity. No one

The possession of troops trained and ready for war, a well-filled treasury and a lively temperament: these were the factors which decided for the war.
—FREDERICK THE GREAT
on the First Silesian War

At the Battle of Fontenoy in May 1745, the British, led by the duke of Cumberland, son of George II, and fortified by Dutch and Saxon forces, were defeated by Prussia's French allies. It was the last battle fought by the British in the War of the Austrian Succession.

imagined that they would try to return home in the dead of winter, but that was exactly what they did — on foot, hauling guns and supplies, leaving 4,000 casualties behind inside Prague. Only about 7,000 of the escapees survived the trek to reach their homeland, and the wounded were released only when their commander, Francois de Chevert, threatened to burn Prague down completely unless they were given a safe-conduct out of the city.

In the meantime Austrian troops commanded by Field Marshal Count Ludwig Andreas Khevenhüller began a counterattack. French and Saxon troops were driven out of Upper Austria, and in December 1741 Khevenhüller swept into Bavaria. By this time,

the electors had flung aside their "guarantees" to comply with the Pragmatic Sanction, and on January 24, 1742, Elector Charles Albert of Bavaria was elected Holy Roman emperor. On February 12, the day he was crowned Emperor Charles VII, the Austrians captured the Bavarian capital of Munich.

Alleging that Maria Theresa had betrayed the Convention of Klein-Schnellendorf by making it public, Frederick had in the meantime returned to the fray. On February 5 he sent his armies into the small country of Moravia. But in this poor nation there was little food to sustain the Prussian army, which also had to contend with Khevenhüller's soldiers and Hungarian reinforcements.

Unable to take the fortress at Brünn because his Saxon allies had no cannon, Frederick retreated to nearby Bohemia. Austrian commander Prince Charles of Lorraine, Maria Theresa's brother-in-law, then tried to intercept the Prussians. The battle that ensued at Chotusitz on May 17 was decisive. Prussian forces numbered 28,000; the Austrians, 28,150. Frederick, however, enjoyed a two-to-one advantage in artillery. His general, Anhalt-Dessau, resisted valiantly but was unable to stop Prince Charles's onslaught. Then Frederick himself went on the attack, destroying the Austrian left flank. Frederick did not give chase when the Austrians fled. The Prussians distinguished themselves in battle and won a decisive victory but suffered 4,000 casualties. The Prussian cavalry had been decimated. About 700 Prussians were missing or taken prisoner. Losses for the unit commanded by Frederick were slight, but the rest of the army suffered higher casualties than had the enemy.

The Prussian victory at Chotusitz brought to a close the First Silesian War, as the conflict between Austria and Prussia for that region is known. The two nations made a separate peace through the Treaty of Breslau in 1742, by which Maria Theresa ceded Silesia to Frederick. The larger European conflict of which the Prussian-Austrian struggle was a part, called the War of the Austrian Succession, continued.

By the spring of 1743, only three years after he

had ascended the throne, Frederick was known to all Europe as a force with which to be reckoned. In fact, of all the combatants in the First Silesian War, only Frederick of Prussia had gotten what he had fought for. Certainly he had secured his reputation as a general, but as a diplomat he was now recognized as unscrupulous by both allies and adversaries. He weakened both the French and the Austrians

Frederick leaves the field after winning the battle of Hohenfriedeberg on June 4, 1745. The first battle planned and executed by the king alone, it was a significant turning point in the Second Silesian War. The Prussian victory and domestic unrest in England encouraged George II to make peace with Prussia.

and for a time secured his claims to Silesia. He had prevented France from becoming "arbiter of the Universe." Ultimately, he had taught the rulers of Europe that he was neither a weakling nor a fool. On this score, their judgments had thus proved to be premature.

Only a year later, however, he was obliged to fight the Second Silesian War. For Maria Theresa had learned not only to respect Frederick but to despise him. Maria Theresa was an intelligent, energetic, and ambitious woman, with many goals. Among other desires, she wanted to be empress of the Holy Roman Empire. She wanted Silesia back, too, for she still believed it was rightfully hers. But what she wanted most — more than anything else in the world — was to defeat Frederick. When the next war was underway she snapped at an British envoy, "And if I had to make peace with him tomorrow, I would still fight him today."

Although Prussia was no longer a participant, the War of the Austrian Succession raged on. Maria Theresa took back Bohemia and once more occupied Bavaria. Frederick's former allies, the French and the Saxons, were being soundly defeated by the Austrians, who had been joined by the British, under the Hanoverian King George II, who were not about to let the French increase their power on the continent. As for Prussia, Frederick believed that fortresses, a large and refurbished army, alliances, and sizeable government revenues would ensure security. "A happy quiescence must be our guiding principle . . . for the next few years; we need peace to consolidate the State," he wrote. With Silesia now part of his realm, Frederick ruled over an additional 2 million people. From the taxes they paid he increased revenues by 4.5 million talers.

In May 1744 Frederick took action against possible adversity. If the conflict between France and Austria ended in French surrender, it could seriously threaten Prussia. First, on May 22, he made a pact with Emperor Charles VII known as the Union of Frankfurt, promising that Bavaria would be his to rule again. On June 4, he concluded another secret treaty with France — the Treaty of Paris. The stage was set for the Second Silesian War.

In 1744 Maria Theresa was allied with both Britain and Holland and was prepared to fight the Prussians. On July 1, 1744, Austrian troops entered the French territories of Alsace and Lorraine. On August 15 Frederick went with Anhalt-Dessau and Schwerin to Bohemia with an army of 80,000 men, an extremely large force for the period. On September 16 their combined forces captured the city of Prague, then proceeded to conquer Bohemia almost entirely. But as winter set in and his armies' supplies began to run out, his soldiers began to desert rather than starve or freeze to death. In Frederick's day, winter put a temporary halt to battle. It was impossible to transport sufficient food and clothing for the men during freezing weather and difficult also to move the heavy artillery pieces through snow. Frederick took advantage of the winter of 1744—45. While all the combatants' forces either went home or into winter quarters, he ordered the royal silver to be melted down to pay for another campaign.

One of Frederick's constant concerns was French foreign policy. To him, France was still the expanding military power it had been under Louis XIV. Actually, France's power was in decline. England, France's rival, had hoped to see the Austrians finish off the troublesome Prussians so they could attack France. In 1743, after leading British and Hanoverian troops against the French in the Battle of Dettingen, George II of Britain had arranged the Treaty of Worms with Austria, Holland, and Sardinia (now part of Italy). Since the First Silesian War, Britain had worried about Prussia's increasing strength. However, in January 1745 Frederick, who had already broken the Treaty of Breslau, had reason to worry: another agreement (the Quadruple Alliance) was reached between the English, Austrians, Dutch, and, this time, the Saxons. He felt then that the war was all the more necessary because of "the evil designs" of the forces arrayed against him.

Frederick's situation seemed as desperate as ever. As defender of the "Liberty of the Empire," Frederick had fought in Bohemia, on behalf of the Holy Roman emperor. On January 20, 1745, Charles VII died. Bavaria then promptly withdrew from hostilities with Austria, agreeing to the Peace of Füssen. Frederick was encouraged however by the outcome of the Battle of Fontenoy (now in Belgium) in May 1745. A French army commanded by Marshal Maurice de Saxe defeated British and Dutch forces, led by the duke of Cumberland, a son of the British king.

The first Prussian victory for which Frederick was wholly responsible was the Battle of Hohenfriedeberg (now Dabromierz in Poland) on June 4. He both planned and executed the strategy. When the Austrians gradually began to gather near the small village, he unleashed his attack. His plan was to fight the Austrians and their Saxon allies separately, thus turning one large battle into two smaller ones. The Prussian cavalry, with orders to give no quarter, inflicted heavy casualties on the Saxons. Soon the Saxons were fleeing for their lives with the Prussians giving chase. When the Austrians finally joined battle, Frederick's infantry charged the Austrian center, managing to break apart the mass of troops. Prince Charles and the Austrian army were defeated. Of the almost 60,000 Prussians involved, those taken prisoner, killed, and wounded numbered 4,751. As for Austria's ally, the Saxons lost 3,400 of their 19,000 troops.

British domestic politics, in the meantime, turned unstable, affecting British foreign policy to Frederick's advantage. Charles Edward Stuart,

known as "the Young Pretender" and "Bonnie Prince Charlie," had landed in the Scottish islands of the Hebrides to press his claim to the British throne. The ensuing revolt was called the Jacobite rebellion. George II now had to deal with a challenge to his reign on his own soil. Furthermore, Frederick's victory at Hohenfriedeberg had strengthened Prussia's diplomatic standing with the British crown. George II was now willing to bargain with Prussia. The result was the Convention of Hanover, which was signed on August 26, 1745. By the terms of the treaty Britain recognized Prussia's occupation of Silesia, while Prussia agreed to recognize Maria Theresa's husband, Francis, as Holy Roman emperor.

Still, Maria Theresa was determined to regain Silesia. Disheartened by the recent disaster at Hohenfriedeberg, the Austrians still had to suffer two more resounding defeats before hostilities came to an end. The Battle of Soor, in Bohemia, was the first of these. In the opening moves before the battle, Prince Charles outfoxed Frederick. The Prussian

Voltaire (left) and Frederick in the garden at Sans Souci. Frederick first wrote to the celebrated author in 1736, and he persuaded him to reside at Sans Souci in 1750. After several bitter disputes with the king, Voltaire left Prussia in 1753.

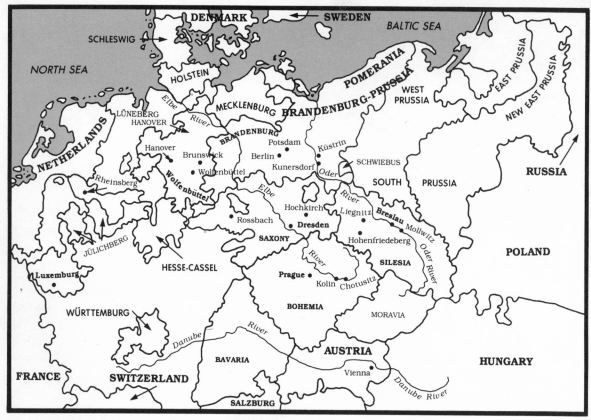

DONNA ESHLEMAN

Brandenburg-Prussia and surrounding states. The Prussia of Frederick the Great was militarily active, fighting in both the War of the Austrian Succession and the Seven Years' War, and added Silesia and part of Poland to its territory.

forces were outmaneuvered, finding themselves facing much larger Austrian regiments. At first Prussian losses were high, but because the Austrians failed to follow up their initial breakthrough, Frederick was able to gain reinforcements. The final blow for the Austrians occurred when Prince Ferdinand of Brunswick and his soldiers arrived and charged into the fray.

Still, Maria Theresa would not relent. The 33-year-old king was nearly beside himself with anxiety. Finally, Prussian grenadiers, trained and commanded by Anhalt-Dessau, battled the Saxons once more — this time on the icy slopes of Kesselsdorf. The odds were not with the Prussians. After a brief prayer, Anhalt-Dessau ordered his troops into the teeth of enemy fire with the cry, "In the name of Jesus, march!" The grenadiers scrambled for the heights as the Saxon cannon cut them down. A slaughter seemed certain until the Saxons inexplicably left their fortified positions and began struggling hand-to-hand with the Prussians on the slopes. The Saxons lost the advantage entirely when their artillery was forced to hold its fire during this tense and puzzling moment. Anhalt-Dessau, seeing that the tables could now be easily turned in his favor, flung his cavalry at the hill. The Saxons' guns were soon seized and their infantry put on the run. The nearby city of Dresden was captured days later. Frederick had won the Second Silesian War.

The Peace of Dresden, signed on Christmas Day 1745, concluded the hostilities between Prussia and Austria, although Austria and the other combatants continued the War of the Austrian Succession until 1748. Once again Maria Theresa had been defeated; once again Frederick had kept Silesia and proved to the world his eminence as a military commander and a diplomat of the first rank. He knew very well that someday he would face Maria Theresa again, but he knew also that it would not be very soon.

Meanwhile, Frederick's own beloved Prussia urgently required his attention; forced to devote his energies to military campaigns, little remained for looking after the internal affairs of his own kingdom. Now he went home both to assume these tasks once more and to build himself a new castle, Sans Souci. The name means "Without Cares," and for a short while that phrase described Frederick's existence. As he rode home to Berlin early in the year 1745, he must have looked forward to quietly governing his kingdom and to spending time at home with friends, enjoying with them his long neglected poetry and music.

In the years following the Second Silesian War Frederick's cherished friendship with Voltaire rapidly became a source of displeasure. Frederick had faithfully corresponded with the eminent French intellectual since 1736. They met briefly just after Frederick took the throne. Frederick was ill and confined to bed at the time. Not until 1750 did Frederick learn how difficult his brilliant friend could be. Frederick invited Voltaire to take up residence in Berlin, and Voltaire accepted. As a result the few years of peace that were to follow were almost as full of drama for Frederick as his war years had been.

5

The Rising Tempest

At Sans Souci, Frederick surrounded himself with the things and people he loved, but even in the midst of luxury he worked very hard. His routine began at 4:00 A.M., and he instructed his servants that if he were not awake at that time they were to throw wet cloths on his face. He at once got dressed in his uniform, which consisted of an ancient blue coat, old black trousers shiny with wear, and battered boots. Thus prepared for the day, he began to work.

One of the criticisms made against Frederick was that he never really learned to delegate duties to other people. This, it has been said, was because, with few exceptions, he did not much respect the intelligence or abilities of others and thought he could do everything better himself. Although there is no doubt that he was enormously intelligent, talented, and efficient, the fact that Frederick insisted on running everything himself made his kingdom vulnerable in an important way. It meant that if anything happened to him, Prussia could fall into chaos. Because he alone kept things running smoothly, there was really no system for keeping things going without him.

The most desirable thing in this world is to live in peace.
—FREDERICK THE GREAT

Frederick sits alone after the shattering defeat inflicted on his forces by the Austrian general Count Leopold von Daun at the battle of Kolin in June 1757. Frederick was victorious at the Battles of Rossbach and Leuthen later that same year.

François Marie Arouet, known as Voltaire, was one of the greatest French writers of the intellectual movement known as the Enlightenment. Frederick took great pleasure in their long and volatile association, although their friendship flourished only when they were apart.

Furthermore, there was little, if any, participation in government by the common people of the kingdom. Under Frederick's system, the ruler was active — he governed — and the people were passive — they were governed. There was always a great deal for Frederick to do: letters to read and answer, decisions to make, orders to give. At mid-morning he directed military exercises. Afterwards he ate his noon meal. In the afternoon he returned to work, then went for a brisk walk. Between projects he practiced his flute and composed music. After a full day he ate supper at 10:00 P.M., and still there was more to do, for he liked to hold concerts at which he could display his musical talent. During this time he received a personal visit from the composer Bach.

Meanwhile, Frederick kept writing to Voltaire, trying to persuade the French wit to come and live at Sans Souci. Convincing Voltaire to take up residence in Prussia was not an easy task, since doing so would force the Frenchman to leave behind two women with whom he was in love: Madame du Châtelet, whom he had known for twenty years, and Madame Denis, his niece, whom he loved with great passion. But Madame du Châtelet had a husband as well as another lover, and Madame Denis, while living with Voltaire in Paris, nevertheless carried on affairs with other men as well. Still, although the great *philosophe* had received the acclaim of his king, Louis XV, he had not been invited to the king's social gatherings. Snubbed by the king of France, Voltaire found the offer from the enthusiastic Prussian king increasingly attractive. "Come and visit me. I promise a fresh crown of the finest laurels," Frederick wrote in 1745.

Frederick (rear, center) and Voltaire (facing Frederick at left) engage in lively conversation at Sans Souci. The two quarreled over Voltaire's satirical attack on another French intellectual, Pierre-Louis Moreau de Maupertuis, a mathematician and astronomer whom Frederick appointed head of Prussia's Academy of Science.

Finally, Voltaire gave in to Frederick's entreaties and moved to Sans Souci in 1750, where he thought he would be better treated. But the two friends did not get along as well at close quarters as they had when they lived in separate countries. Frederick liked to tease his friends, and sometimes he hurt their feelings severely without realizing it. He had a tendency to make people feel insecure, playing one off against another for the pleasure of watching their uncomfortable reactions. As it turned out, Voltaire was sensitive to such behavior and, after all, he had come to Sans Souci at Frederick's request.

For his part, Voltaire was brilliant, cultured, well-read, and wonderfully entertaining, but he was also egotistical, devious, a gossip, and sarcastic. He tended also to believe that people were plotting against him. Despite this quirk of Voltaire's, Frederick seems to have given the Frenchman substantial reason to wonder about his welcome. Voltaire also was a trifle greedy and indeed was not above participating in questionable financial dealings if he could profit from them. When he got the chance to take part in an illegal transaction involving German currency, he did so, despite the embarrassment he knew it would cause Frederick. Voltaire also disapproved of Pierre-Louis Moreau de Maupertuis, whom he ridiculed in a satire entitled *Doctor Akakia*. Maupertuis served Frederick as president of Prussia's Academy of Sciences. Voltaire accused his countryman of being a sham. On presenting the manuscript to Frederick, Voltaire and the king read it aloud. At several points it was thrown into the fire and snatched from the flames before it was finally burned. Voltaire led the king to believe that the work was not to be published. Frederick very much enjoyed the joke and danced gleefully in front of the fireplace with Voltaire. What the king did not know was that his friend had every intention of publishing the work. The writer ignored the probable embarrassment it would cause not only Maupertuis but also the scholar's patron — Frederick the Great. Once printed, the book was thus confiscated by the king, who reproached Voltaire, telling him "that if your works deserve statues, your conduct deserves

Voltaire with Madame de Pompadour, mistress of Louis XV of France. Her dislike for Frederick helped bring about France's alliance with Austria, part of the Diplomatic Revolution, both crucial steps toward the Seven Years' War.

chains." As the conflict between them escalated, it received increasing public attention. Voltaire's satire found its way into more and more editions; Frederick discovered a copy printed in Leipzig and was so outraged he had it publicly burned. In fact, the incident deteriorated into a sordid public scandal, and after the lawsuit that followed, Frederick sent Voltaire away to live at Berlin.

Finally, the two settled their differences, and Voltaire returned to Sans Souci, but not to live in the palace. Instead, Frederick built Voltaire a house nearby, an arrangement that did not prevent their quarrelling even more furiously. Frederick invited Voltaire to parties and then ignored him. Voltaire made cruel remarks about Frederick and made certain that Frederick heard about them.

The public is a ferocious beast; one must either chain it up or flee from it.
—VOLTAIRE
French philosopher

Frederick and his generals watch the French armies at Rossbach trying to surround them. After winning the battle, the king slept in a pantry so as not to disturb wounded French officers quartered in the same castle.

THE BETTMANN ARCHIVE

As the two men's tempers smoldered over these matters, their friendship cooled. Voltaire stayed for a time at Potsdam, but he barely caught sight of the king, who now shunned him. After requesting a leave of absence because of illness, Voltaire left the Prussian court in March 1753. He did so carrying certain items, including some of Frederick's verses, which the king had expressly asked to have returned before Voltaire's departure. On reaching the city of Frankfurt, Voltaire found that the Prussian ruler had given orders that he be detained there until he handed over the things the king demanded. Unluckily, Voltaire had left the manuscripts in Hamburg. A subsequent attempt to escape from Frankfurt only landed the great French author in jail. Finally, the verses with which the king was so concerned were restored to their royal owner, and Voltaire continued on his way.

Meanwhile, the political situation in Europe was becoming increasingly stormy since Maria Theresa still longed to win a war against the Prussian king, and it had begun to appear as though Russia might form an alliance with her. Between 1749 and 1756 a great diplomatic reversal took place. Previous alliances were swept aside as nations allied themselves with their former enemies. This diplomatic switch is sometimes called "the Diplomatic Revolution." Maria Theresa and Louis XV of France came to a secret treaty agreement. Thus, in a reversal of alliances the French, who had been allied with Frederick, switched to the Austrian side, and the British, previously Austria's allies, to Frederick's side. (In fact, Frederick became so prominent in England that a china factory there began producing mugs on which the Prussian king was portrayed with cherubs holding a wreath above his head.) In January 1756 Frederick signed the Treaty of Westminster, thus agreeing that neither Prussia nor England would fight against any German state.

Prussian General Friedrich von Seydlitz (center) outflanked and defeated the larger French arm at Rossbach. Before attacking, the Prussians waited until the French spread their troops too thinly. Voltaire remarked that the Prussian victory marked the birth of German nationalism.

England declared war on France on May 17. Frederick had feared possible Russian aggression ever since Empress Elizabeth had approved an agreement with England to station troops on the Prussian border in September 1755. Russia, in turn, grew frightened about Prussian motives following Frederick's diplomatic arrangements with England.

The Treaty of Versailles, signed between France and Austria in May, formalized the arrangement by which Frederick would end up fighting not only the Austrians and the French but the huge Russian armies as well. On August 26, 1756, believing the Austrians and their allies were about to attack him, Frederick occupied Dresden, located in Saxony, halfway between the Prussian capital, Berlin, and the Austrian-controlled city of Prague.

Upon taking Dresden, Frederick's soldiers pushed the Saxon queen through a doorway in order to seize some papers. The action infuriated European royalty, especially Louis XV of France, for the Saxon queen's daughter was Louis's daughter-in-law. In response, Louis sent four times as many men against Frederick as he had originally promised Maria Theresa — 100,000 in all. But Frederick solidified his control of Saxony at the Battles of Lobositz and Pirna, capturing the Saxon army and nearly 100 artillery pieces. Prussia now could collect taxes from that particularly wealthy nation. He spent the winter in Dresden, then in the spring of 1757 marched on toward Prague, where he engaged the Austrians in a ferocious battle.

Although Frederick was victorious in this early bout of fighting, it was a bitter gain. His friend Schwerin, who had helped save the day in the Battle of Mollwitz, had been killed. The dead and wounded numbered in the tens of thousands. Perhaps worst of all, 400 officers died, a grievous loss, since well-trained officers were not easily replaced. Six weeks later, while still laying siege to Prague, he suffered another horrendous defeat.

At the Battle of Kolin, Daun, Maria Theresa's trusted general, led his combined army of 53,000 soldiers to the Elbe River, not far from Prague. Instead of maintaining his superiority in numbers,

Frederick split his own army in two. He thought Daun could be subdued with a force numbering only 35,000. After striking at the Austrian right flank, the Prussians were attacked by light infantry units, causing surprisingly high losses. The cost to Frederick was bloody; he lost 12,000 men while Daun lost only 8,000. Frederick retreated into Saxony and was forced to let go his grip on Prague.

Frederick's astute strategy and confusion among the Austrian commanders led to the Prussian victory at the Battle of Leuthen on December 5, 1757. The Prussians won decisively despite being badly outnumbered.

On top of this misfortune, on July 2, 1757, he received word that his mother, Sophia Dorothea, had died. He then plunged into the blackest despair. At home, he had thought he might win this war, but now he was surrounded by armies that made his own look insignificant. The only factor that prevented the Russians from completely destroying his forces was that they kept running out of supplies, which forced them to return to Russia periodically rather than advance against their enemy. He feared being killed, but more than that he feared being taken prisoner and forced to give orders from captivity, orders that would bring beloved Prussia to its knees. It was at this time that Frederick wrote once again to Voltaire, still his friend despite all that had transpired. The sentiment was one that ruled Frederick's life: "In the face of the storm and the threat of shipwreck I must think, live, and die like a king."

Frederick surprises Austrian officers in the town of Lissa, shortly after the Prussian victory at the Battle of Leuthen, later called a military masterpiece by Napoleon. At Lissa the Prussian king discovered the houses full of deserters from the Austrian and allied armies.

It was not idle talk; he meant it and his actions showed that he was determined to live up to this motto. Never one to lie in bed, he nearly stopped sleeping entirely now. He had no time for rest. Frederick had to scramble to keep his armies supplied; only the personal devotion of his soldiers kept them fighting at all, for certainly circumstances looked almost hopeless.

At this time, Frederick was also receiving financial and military help from the English. George II placed an "army of observation" in the western German states to interfere with French attempts to enter the region. England also made further trouble for the French by raiding their coasts and challenging them over colonial territory in North America.

Despite this assistance, the French, Russians, and Austrians were all on the move. In whatever direction of the compass he faced, Frederick saw his adversaries advancing, closing in for the kill. England had already suffered several military setbacks. Especially disappointing was the French victory at Hastenbeck in June of 1757 against Hanoverian troops commanded by the duke of Cumberland. The Prussians, Frederick knew, had to break out of the stranglehold before it was too late. In November Frederick marched a small army of 22,000 men to the village of Rossbach, near Leipzig. There, he and General Friedrich von Seydlitz confronted 41,000 French troops. The French commander chose a sweeping movement to cut off the Prussians. But like a nimble David against a lumbering Goliath, Frederick suddenly went on the attack and knocked the French off balance. Prussian artillery and cavalry did their lethal work, and the French offensive was shattered. The French lost 8,000 men, while the Prussians were nearly unscathed with fewer than 600 casualties.

After another defeat at the Silesian town of Breslau (now Wroclaw in Poland), Frederick again needed a brilliant military success. He also wanted to recover Breslau. On December 5, Daun and Prince Charles, with 72,000 Austrians, met Frederick's exhausted and tattered 30,000 troops, on their way from Liegnitz. Using the heaviest artillery

Count Daun and the Austrians defeated Frederick decisively at Kolin in June 1757. Frederick made the error of splitting his forces and ruining his advantage in numbers. At Hochkirch, in October 1758, Daun's surprise attack on Frederick's encampment killed many Prussians in the early morning darkness.

Elizabeth Petrovna, empress of Russia, was one of Frederick's most menacing adversaries. Her death saved Prussia from certain defeat in the Seven Years' War when her successor, the mad Tsar Peter III, stopped Russia's war against Frederick.

he could muster, Frederick smashed the Austrian defenses. His infantry then concentrated on a single point along the Austrian line. The Austrian infantry collapsed, and their cavalry were sent running. Thus ended the Battle of Leuthen (now Lutynia, in southwestern Poland); 6,000 Austrians were killed, and another 20,000 surrendered.

Severe misfortune awaited Frederick, however, in March 1758. An important shipment of supplies for Frederick's forces was captured by the Austrians. There followed a series of unsuccessful battles, culminating in the massacre at Hochkirch on October 14, 1758, where the Austrians stormed into Frederick's camp just before dawn and attacked the Prussians, who were still asleep in their tents. Units not wiped out in the assault struggled on alone. The attacks divided the Prussians into smaller groups, while their custom had always been to fight in single large formations. However, Frederick had risked just such a dangerous situation by camping in the open, and Daun, the Austrian commander, had seized the opportunity. Refusing to retreat, Frederick managed to rally his terrified soldiers. Nonetheless, Hochkirch was a serious defeat for the Prussians, who lost over a quarter of their forces.

Three days later, on October 17, Frederick received word that his dear sister Wilhelmina had died after a long illness. Of everyone in his life, he loved her most. She had been his friend since the days of his difficult childhood. He had written her nearly every day for years. Most of his friends had already died and now Wilhelmina, his oldest and perhaps closest friend, was gone.

Frederick's emotional loss was compounded by his deteriorating health. The rigors of 18th-century warfare might have killed a younger, healthier man, yet Frederick's tremendous will had enabled him to continue his rule and command. With his usual flintiness, he faced the truth, describing himself in a letter: "If you could see me, you would detect no trace of my former self." He was now "a man turned old and grey, minus half his teeth and quite without gaity, fire or imagination, in brief, a shadow." Besides stomach pains, he had gout, rheumatism, headache, toothache, chills, and fevers. After the nightmare of Hochkirch, Frederick tried reading aloud from the tragedy *Mithridate* by the French playwright Jean Racine. But perhaps the pain was too great this time for a man even of the king's measured self-restraint. The king who once had pardoned a mentally disturbed soldier for attempting to commit suicide now appeared to be considering taking his own life. He revealed a small oval box to his friend and secretary Heinrich de Catt. It contained opium pills, which, the king explained, were "amply sufficient to send one to the sombre shore where there is no return."

By August 1759 things looked very bleak indeed. The French and Austrians, believing they would

Frederick the Great in danger of being captured by the feared Russian cavalrymen, the Cossacks, during the Seven Years' War. At times the military situation appeared so bleak for Frederick and the Prussians that he contemplated suicide.

win, had signed a new treaty; in addition, the Austrians and Russians had nearly reached the city of Berlin and would take it if they were not stopped. Russians and Hungarians committed atrocities against civilian populations in the towns they occupied. The English, although they sent Frederick the money they promised, did nothing more to help him. The battle at Kunersdorf on August 12, 1759, was disastrous. The combined forces of the Russian Field Marshal Peter Saltykov and the Austrian General Laudon smashed Frederick's offensive. Against overwhelming odds the badly outnumbered Prussians nearly won, but at the last moment the tide of battle turned, when the Russians and Austrians obtained more guns and reinforcements. He rode from the scene of disaster and cried, "I am lost." He admitted in a letter to Voltaire there was no "pleasure in this dog's life, in seeing and procuring the killing of individuals personally unknown to me."

There was nothing he could do now but prepare for the fall of Berlin, but the Austrians and Russians did not move at once. Instead, believing they could finish Frederick off any time they wished, they took their time, and Frederick was able to take advantage of their overconfidence. He managed to prevent French and Russian forces from retaking Silesia, and by then it was winter once again and the Russians went home to replenish their supplies. While the French and Austrians were in their own winter quarters, Frederick raced to assemble a ragged band of 100,000 badly supplied and all but untrained soldiers. When spring came he faced a renewed Russian and Austrian offensive and expected little else but defeat. Still, under his leadership the Prussians persisted and survived the terrible August at Liegnitz, thanks to the drunken deserter who warned him of the Austrian surprise attack.

With respect to warfare, it seemed at times that Frederick valued nothing more highly than bravery and discipline. He is said to have answered a mortally wounded soldier's last moans on the battlefield: "Die quietly, can't you!" During one battle, at the sight of his troops hesitating to repel an Austrian attack, he cursed, "Rogues, would you live forever!"

Tsar Peter III of Russia had almost unlimited admiration for Prussia and Frederick. One Saxon minister lamented, "The king of Prussia is now Emperor of Russia" after Empress Elizabeth's death. By June 1762 Russian troops were fighting their former Austrian allies.

The failure of the Austrian ploy at Liegnitz greatly inspired Frederick's men. Yet only two months later, they were horrified to learn that Berlin had at last fallen to the Austrians and the Russians. The occupiers fled upon Frederick's approach and 65,000 of Maria Theresa's soldiers, again led by Daun, took up positions near Torgau, south of Berlin on the Elbe River. On November 3 Frederick advanced on the Austrian fortifications with 44,000 men. Using a cavalry charge to distract the enemy, his own troops tried to encircle Daun's position from behind. The cavalrymen were nearly annihilated. By accepting heavy losses and continuously sending in reinforcements, Frederick managed to crack the Austrian lines by nightfall. Daun was defeated. It had been an unusually savage battle, however, and both sides suffered enormous casualties.

Frederick is mobbed by curious peasants while riding through a village. He took a detached view of his popularity, quipping: "Put an old monkey on a horse . . . they would do just the same." Following the Seven Years' War, the people of Silesia were impressed by Frederick's speedy efforts to rebuild the region.

Although he won the Battle of Torgau, Frederick felt the end was near, and when the fighting slacked off again for the winter, he said that everything seemed as black as if he were already in his tomb. And 1761 seemed to prove him right: the Prussians and their allies lost nearly every battle they fought, most importantly the Battle of Schweidnitz in October. Frederick's own army was too small and ill-provisioned even to take the field. With the Austrians on one side, the Russians on the other, and the French ready to swoop down the middle whenever they were inclined to, real defeat was at hand. The whole of Germany was so full of Frederick's enemies that he could not obtain men, horses, or supplies. Every town and hamlet was occupied by enemy soldiers.

The age of miracles is over, Frederick said. He once again seriously considered suicide. He had fought valiantly, while ruining what remained of his own health and impoverishing his country to fuel the war effort. The triumph of the superior forces massed against him was only a matter of time.

But then an astonishing thing happened, one that no one could have predicted: just as they were about to be overrun, Frederick and Prussia were saved by the death of Empress Elizabeth of Russia on January 5, 1762.

While Elizabeth had been Frederick's enemy, her successor was her nephew Karl Peter Ulrich, duke of Holstein-Gottorp, who loved and admired Frederick with the intensity of a madman — which in fact he was. In his madness, this tsar, known as Peter III, immediately ordered the Russian troops in Germany to change sides and fight for Frederick. In addition, Peter ordered all Russian forces occupying Prussian lands to give those lands back to Frederick. While the orders could be judged insane, no Russian soldier or general was prepared to disobey the tsar of Russia. Mad though he might be, he was still capable of ordering them put to death if they dared to defy him.

The result was the end, almost at once, of the Seven Years' War. With the Russian withdrawal, Sweden also made peace. Although France and Austria continued as combatants, both were too exhausted by their losses to pursue the war with much zeal. The Prussians recaptured Schweidnitz and were victorious at Freiberg in October 1762. Maria Theresa, the empress of the Holy Roman Empire of the German Nations, was forced to admit that she had met her match in the king of Prussia. By the peace treaty of Hubertusburg, on February 15, 1763, Frederick retained Silesia. Great Britain was the only real victor, having won control of Canada and India in large part because Frederick had kept the French so busy fighting in Europe.

At age 51, bent and tired, Frederick returned to Berlin amidst cheering crowds, to face a task at least as big as the war had been: setting about the reconstruction of his war-damaged nation. The kingdom's industry, agriculture, trade, and population had all been ravaged by years of war and were badly in need of his attentions.

> *There are no laurels for the lazy.*
> —FREDERICK THE GREAT

fig. 5

fig. 6

fig. 7

fig. 1.   b

fig. 4

6

The Enlightened Absolutist

When Frederick returned to Berlin in 1763, victorious at least in the eyes of the citizenry, he knew that his only victory had been surviving until the death of the empress of Russia. Avoiding the celebration his subjects had prepared for him, he crept secretly into town and shut himself up in the palace. But his isolation did not last long; almost at once he began to put his battered kingdom back on its feet.

Once again his eye for detail and thirst for information served him well. He had, after all, been riding around his own kingdom on horseback for seven years, and, typically, little escaped his notice. Now he spoke to his ministers about the deficiencies in agriculture, of the industries most likely to succeed in different parts of the land, the need for new products to balance Prussia's trade deficits, and the need for immigrants to settle underused territory. He saw everything, and did something about all of it.

His energy was such that to him few achievements were impossible.
—W. F. REDDAWAY
British historian, on Frederick

A European rural scene illustrates 18th century agricultural techniques. Between the Second Silesian War and the Seven Years' War, Frederick successfully increased Prussia's agricultural productivity. By annexing Silesia, Frederick added 2 million people to his realm and found a new source of tax revenues.

First, he decided to give 35,000 army horses to the peasants. Next, he earmarked the remainder of his war treasury for the rebuilding of his kingdom. He set up a marketing system whereby excess produce could be sold; when produce was scarce, he subsidized farmers, and when it was plentiful, the government helped keep prices high by buying some of it and finding other customers for the rest. He

An elderly Frederick inspects the building of a dam in East Prussia. As well as trying to improve his subjects' lives, he encouraged religious freedom and free speech, once even allowing the display of a cartoon criticizing his frugal economic policies.

instituted crop rotation, selective livestock breeding, and soil improvement programs. He promoted planting of potatoes and sugar beets, two crops he knew would help stave off famine in years when grain harvests were poor. Meanwhile, he struggled to rebuild the army, which by now was nearly nonexistent and had to be staffed and trained from scratch.

In everything I say, I affect the air of thinking of nothing but the happiness of my subjects.
—FREDERICK THE GREAT

Frederick visits a Prussian textile factory. His practice of personally running the kingdom upset many nobles. The Prussian people, however, thought highly of him even though they disliked his tax system, which was administered by French bureaucrats.

At Berlin, he started a china factory as well as a thriving fabrics manufacturing industry. Soon, Prussian-made wools, silks, cottons, and linens found a market. In Silesia he began a mining industry which, after a slow start, became quite successful.

His determination to do everything himself was at once his strong point and his greatest flaw. For when only one man understands how the country is being run, as was the case during Frederick's reign, then the absence of that one man can cause the downfall of his system. Furthermore, even while Frederick insisted that in his kingdom there should be complete freedom of speech, he now began to depart somewhat from that rule. Public criticism of the tax system and critical comment on the military were disallowed. Even religious freedom was curtailed when, as sometimes happened, religious controversy grew so heated that Frederick deemed it an internal danger to the state.

Frederick, with the best motives, could be extremely stubborn, even tyrannical. Still, he did not exercise such tyranny for personal reasons; once, in fact, when he was out riding he saw some of his subjects raising a critical caricature of him. The caricature depicted a miserly Frederick taking great care while grinding coffee not to lose a single bean. When the king approached and inspected the picture, his subjects looked on, fearful of his reaction. Instead of tearing it down, he ordered that it be posted lower so that more people could see it.

Meanwhile, even with all the repairs he was busily making within Prussia, he still had to pay attention to the affairs of neighboring powers. He knew that peace treaties alone could not keep Prussia from war if her enemies decided they wanted one. On April 11, 1764, he signed a treaty with the new Russian empress, Catherine the Great, who had deposed her husband, Peter III. In it she agreed to back Prussia's claim to Silesia, since Russian and Austrian resistance had failed to take it away. The treaty also promised Prussia some reward if it had to intervene on Russia's behalf in Poland. Frederick did not put much faith in the treaty. After all, it was said Catherine was involved in the murder of the unfortunate Peter III and the former Tsar Ivan VI, who was Frederick's nephew, all in order to further her ambition

A Prussian silk and embroidery patchwork from the 18th century. Under Frederick's close supervision, the manufacture of textiles became Prussia's most successful industry. In Prussia, 900 new villages were constructed during Frederick's reign, and he reclaimed arable land for forests and farming.

of becoming empress herself. Frederick felt he had plenty of reason to mistrust her — or, rather, he trusted her to do whatever she thought was best for herself, with or without a treaty.

Thus Frederick worked to make Prussia strong, in order not to be dependent on any other country for help. He also thought hard about the matter of his successor, for a man as constantly ill as he was could not help but realize that he would someday die. The heir to the Prussian throne was, unfortunately, his nephew Prince Frederick William, a handsome and amiable but rather dull young man who loved women and children but had no head for ruling a kingdom. Frederick abhorred the notion of passing Prussia on to him, but there was little he could do about it. To Frederick, political murder was out of the question. Prussia was stuck with Frederick William. (He would rule as Frederick William II.) The heir to the Prussian throne would prove to be a weak leader, given to appointing unscrupulous and self-serving advisers. By the time of Frederick William II's death in 1797, the Prussian economy had all but collapsed, the monarchy's officials had become inept, and the military had grown soft.

But soon Frederick's attention was forcibly turned to more immediate problems, for by 1765, with Prussian reconstruction well under way, the volatile European political scene once again threatened to erupt into war. Maria Theresa's son Joseph II became Holy Roman emperor, and Frederick had to think about what the new young ruler might take it into his head to do. Perhaps he remembered when he himself had been a young king and anxious to make a name for himself by invading and conquering neighboring territory. Surely Maria Theresa would not object if her son gave Frederick a bit of trouble by which to remember her. In 1769, though, after the Turks had attacked Russia, Frederick met with the young emperor. It did not seem prudent for the two to be thinking of going to war against each other with the powerful nation of Russia looming over both of them. Indeed, Catherine listened with concern to the rumors that Frederick and Joseph had discussed a treaty of neutrality.

The 1772 partition of Poland by Russia, Prussia, and Austria is represented allegorically in this painting, showing Frederick (far right), Holy Roman Emperor Joseph II (second from right), King Stanislaw II of Poland, and Empress Catherine the Great of Russia.

Joseph II, the son of Maria Theresa and the Holy Roman Emperor Francis I, seen here with his children, succeeded his father as emperor. He also wanted to subdue Frederick and planned the War of the Bavarian Succession against the aging Prussian monarch.

However, it was also said that Frederick and Joseph spent much time at their two meetings poring over maps of Poland. The next year, Prince Henry, Frederick's brother, visited Catherine, and there, too, Poland was discussed. Rumor had it that the Austrians had already seized some territory in that kingdom, supposedly to prevent plague from spreading there. Catherine thought the Austrian move was a wonderful idea and suggested that the Russians and Prussians follow suit. Austria, Prussia, and Russia each took over a part of Poland, an aggressive move that allowed each of Poland's neighbors to seize territory without any of them having to go to war. It may also have helped heal the rift between Frederick and Maria Theresa, for she was against the partition and probably respected Frederick for taking only a small portion of Poland when he could easily have grabbed more. His restraint was considerable in view of his statement that there was nothing else like Poland in Europe and that in its undeveloped wildness it was comparable only to Canada.

His affection for Poland is understandable when we remember how eager Frederick was to improve things, for Poland was an extremely poor and backward nation. In a letter to Voltaire in 1773, Frederick listed some of the things he had done in his new Polish territory: abolished serfdom, reformed the laws, opened a canal to join the main rivers, rebuilt towns, drained marshes, organized a police force, and begun a new system of education.

The law and legal reform had been a longstanding interest of Frederick's. In Prussia, legal reforms had begun as early as 1747, when the kingdom's first judiciary was established, based upon the *Codex Fredericianus* (Frederician code), although it was not until eight years after his death that the complete legal system, called the *Landrecht*, went into effect.

Also among Frederick's new programs for his country was a system of tax reform. The *Regie*, as the new tax system was known, was much criticized; it was modelled on the French system and run by French bureaucrats. Although the new taxes were extremely severe, the government's revenues greatly increased. The national treasury increased from the 8 million talers he controlled at the beginning of his reign to more than 50 million.

By 1775 much of his great energy had left him. His health, never good, had declined to a shocking degree, and the rumor that he was dying spread throughout Europe. At the news, Joseph II prepared to take Silesia back from Prussia as soon as Frederick was dead, but Frederick recovered yet again. In 1777 he again readied an army to fight the Austrians, this time because the Austrians planned to take Bavaria. Although Bavaria did not belong to Frederick, he thought that its defeat by Austria would leave the Austrians entirely too powerful. By April 1778 Frederick was getting ready for the War of the Bavarian Succession, or "potato war."

Maria Theresa's death in 1780 was a blow to Frederick, who said she had honored both her throne and her sex. Now Austrian ambitions to retake Silesia had no restraint. To protect himself against Joseph, in 1785 Frederick formed a confederation of German princes, known as the *Fürstenbund*.

Emperor Joseph was indeed eager to show off his power, but serious conflict never developed, mainly because Russia and Turkey were on good terms, which alarmed Joseph's mother, Maria Theresa. Although Joseph was the emperor, Maria Theresa still had plenty of influence and ability to persuade. In addition, she and Frederick had been adversaries for many years. Without letting Joseph know, she wrote to Frederick, telling him that the German kingdoms had better not fight amongst each other when such huge forces as the Russians and Turks could threaten them with invasion. But the Prussian king saw the need to act against Joseph. Frederick massed 80,000 troops in Silesia, ready to invade Bohemia. No longer confident of his own military abilities, he put Prince Henry in charge. After the Prussians occupied Bohemia from July to October 1778, little happened besides jockeying for position. By May 1779 the crisis was ended through the Peace of Teschen. The Austrians settled for the small district of Burghausen rather than most of Bavaria.

Even in old age Frederick insisted on working as hard as ever. But when Holy Roman Emperor Joseph II instigated the War of the Bavarian Succession, Frederick had to allow his brother Prince Henry to oversee the army.

The king was now 66 years old, old by the standard of the 18th century, in which the average lifespan was years shorter than today. Only 50 years earlier, bubonic plague had killed 300,000 of his subjects. He never trusted physicians, but the doctors of that day had little to offer him. There were no antibiotics. The first vaccinations were still just being developed. There were few painkillers. Dentistry was primitive, and infected teeth were actually a common cause of death. As we have seen, Frederick was never one to sit around coddling his health. Year after year he got up early and stayed up late, maintaining the discipline of his work despite miseries that would have driven another man to his sickbed. He wore his boots even when his feet were swollen with gout. He rode his horse when his entire body ached with rheumatism. In war and peace he maintained his breakneck schedule, pushing his body and health to answer the demands of his implacable will.

Johann Wolfgang von Goethe was the first great German Romantic novelist, poet, and playwright. Generally considered the greatest writer Germany ever produced, Goethe did not meet with the approval of Frederick, who had little regard for German literature.

Perhaps it was unlucky for him that another battle never arose, for when he went home it was to fight against an enemy less merciful than the Austrians. Death lurked in the lovely gardens of Sans Souci now and held court in Berlin. It took Frederick's old friends one by one: his advisers, his few remaining old generals. When it took Voltaire in 1778, it delivered a blow to Frederick that could never be healed, for after the delightful but quarrelsome French wit went to his grave, a set of his memoirs was discovered. In them, Voltaire had written cruel and bitter things about Frederick, mocking him and making terribly hurtful jokes that wounded Frederick's feelings very much. Frederick had thought the old arguments forgotten, and he had believed that hurt feelings had been replaced by forgiveness. Now it seemed that Voltaire had been mocking him all along, even at the end.

In fact, it is not clear that Voltaire ever intended his memoirs to be published. He may have believed that he destroyed the only copies. But for whatever reason, they were published. These writings left Frederick bitter. While he had missed his dead friend, it seemed to him that he had never really had that friend at all, only a secret, clever enemy.

In 1780, another of his adversaries, Maria Theresa of Austria, died. He must have missed her almost as much as he did his friends, for he knew that of all the European leaders, she was one of the few who equalled him in cleverness and ambition. He said himself that although they fought, he never was her enemy and that he respected her. Her son, the Emperor Joseph, went on maneuvering and trying to get the better of Frederick, who was forced to spend his time blocking Joseph's tirelessly devious ambitions.

In 1785, at age 73, Frederick made his last important contribution to Prussian foreign policy. On July 23, 1785, an agreement called the *Fürstenbund*, or the League of Princes, was signed. It established an alliance between Protestant German princes and Catholic ecclesiastical states. Fourteen states in all joined together to resist Joseph's attempt to exchange the Austrian Netherlands for all

> *This woman's achievements were those of a great man.*
> —FREDERICK THE GREAT
> on Maria Theresa of Austria

THE BETTMANN ARCHIVE

Frederick's greyhounds continued to be a source of happiness to him in his final days. Here he watches them play in the forecourt of Sans Souci. The king's last words had to do with what time he planned to get up. He also gestured that he wanted a blanket for one of his dogs.

of Bavaria. Prussia, Saxony, and Hanover formed the core of the league against Austria.

The Prussian king still insisted on supervising the army's practices himself, but while doing this he caught cold. It was a final blow, although as usual he refused to admit how ill he was. The cold developed into chronic breathing difficulties, asthma, and what seemed to be sinus infections. Gasping and tortured by headache, he sat up night after night, unable to catch his breath enough to fall asleep. He was at Sans Souci, where there were no stoves, and he wanted to move to Potsdam, where it was warmer. But he refused to go in a carriage and waited in vain to get better so that he could ride his horse.

Frederick did not get better; he got worse. Finally he had to be taken by carriage, but he insisted that he go in the middle of the night so that no one would see him in such bad condition. By spring, he had improved enough to return to Sans Souci, where he was able to work, have visitors, and even go riding. Still, he knew that he would soon die, and so did everyone else.

One day, after a particularly high fever, he awoke at 5:00 in the morning and began working. But the next day he slept late, an unheard-of indulgence for him, and none of the servants would rouse him; they knew that as soon as he awoke his suffering would begin anew. He tried to give orders to one of his generals, but the general could only stand before him and weep. The rest of the day he spent alternately waking and dozing. Through the night his servant held him up so that he could breathe. His last gasping order was for someone to give his dog a blanket, because it was cold. Even as he was dying, he could not stop trying to repair whatever problem he saw.

A painting by C. B. Rode depicts the scene: Frederick, wearing his shabby old uniform and battered boots, leans in a chair by a blazing hearth, a blanket wrapped around him, his servant supporting his shoulder. By his side on a table is a book by Voltaire; his sword lies by his feet. In the early hours of August 17, 1786, the servant allowed his master's spent body to fall back into the chair, for the fight was over. Frederick was at peace. Only four days earlier he had dictated a letter to a tax official, asking the official to include more details in his report.

Those who were close to him recalled that, after his death, the atmosphere in the palace was one of relief. Frederick himself had said that he had lived too long. Probably during his last years he became increasingly difficult if not tyrannical, capable of issuing orders that were arbitrary and even cruel. His suffering had gone on for a long time, and it must have been a relief to everyone when his agonies were finally at an end. When it became clear that Frederick must soon die, the people naturally looked forward to a younger successor.

The reign of Frederick is a great example of the results of doctrines of efficiency carried to the nth power without scruples or limitations, or consideration for the rights of others.
—GEORGE HAVEN PUTNAM
British historian

Frederick's death was a tremendously solemn and important event in the lives of his subjects, and thousands of people attended his funeral. He had been their ruler for 46 years. He had taken a backward kingdom and turned it into a political, industrial, and military force, not only among the German nations but throughout all Europe.

He did it by following his own greatest rule: Man is made to work, he said, and Frederick worked, serving his beloved Prussian state, right up until the day before his death. Johann Gottfried von Herder, the great German folklorist and philosopher of history, once wrote, "Idleness is the original sin of mankind." Frederick, it can easily be said, was seldom idle.

The death of Frederick on August 17, 1786. After defeating the Prussians in 1806—07, French Emperor Napoleon visited the grave of Frederick, saying that if Frederick had been alive, the French would not have set foot on Prussian soil.

Frederick the Great was a statesman whose abilities were as varied as his insights were profound. From the outset of his reign, he strived personally to guide and remake the Prussian economy and strengthen his nation through the ruthless power struggles of 18th-century Europe. His foreign policy was ruled by the sword and, according to his adversaries, by deceit. Yet, in his day, he proved to be a humanitarian who showed tolerance and patience, stating, "All religions must be tolerated . . . because here everyone must seek salvation after his own way of thinking."

Frederick was a complex individual in a complicated era. Often at war with the French on the battlefield, he was an admirer of their culture. He actually ignored German writers such as Herder, Gotthold Lessing, Christoph Wieland, Friedrich Klopstock, and Johann Wolfgang von Goethe. To the distaste of many, he trusted in French administrators to carry out a tax system that originated in France. His understanding of Enlightenment philosophy was ultimately incomplete. Unlike the French writers he so much admired, he could not bring himself to be optimistic concerning human nature. Frederick was convinced that the majority of humanity was "foolish and bad." He also clung to his belief in predestination, thus contradicting the new and radical ideas of human freedom that sprang up in the 1700s. To Frederick, it was foolhardy for an individual to defy his king or those in power. These feelings, however, did not stop him from writing:

> If my soul like Thebes had a hundred doors
> I would bid joys enter in tens and scores.

While he refused to be a despot, he could not relinquish authority over any aspect of the state. Thus he required strict obedience in order to execute plans he felt were wise and intended to benefit his people. Frederick thought that if the king must serve the state, then so must his people. He was an absolutist who tried to bring together the statecraft of a German prince with the intelligence of an Enlightenment thinker.

Frederick considered it a serious and sacred obligation to give his subjects the greatest measure of happiness, material well-being, intellectual vitality, and moral energy that could be combined with the purposes of the state.
—FRIEDRICH MEINECKE
German historian

Further Reading

Aldington, R. *The Letters of Voltaire and Frederick the Great.* New York: Brendon & Sons, 1927.

Carlyle, Thomas. *The History of Frederick the Great of Prussia.* Chicago: University of Chicago Press, 1969.

Duffy, Christopher. *The Army of Frederick the Great.* Pomfret, VT: David & Charles, 1974.

Durant, Will, and Ariel Durant. *The Age of Voltaire.* New York: Simon & Schuster, 1965.

Gooch, G. P. *Frederick the Great: The Ruler, the Writer, the Man.* New York: Archon Books, 1947.

Mitford, Nancy. *Frederick the Great.* New York: Harper & Row, 1970.

Simon, Edith. *The Making of Frederick the Great.* Boston: Little, Brown, 1963.

Chronology

Jan. 24, 1712	Born Frederick Hohenzollern to King Frederick William of Brandenburg-Prussia and Queen Sophia Dorothea
1730	Frederick's plans to escape to France are discovered; he is imprisoned at Küstrin
June 12, 1733	Marries Princess Elizabeth Christina of Brunswick-Bevern
1740	Frederick William dies; Frederick ascends Prussian throne
1740–42	First Silesian War; Frederick conquers Silesia
1744	Frederick signs the Treaty of Paris; the Second Silesian War begins
June 1745	Defeats Austrian and Saxon forces at Hohenfriedeberg
Dec. 1745	Peace of Dresden concludes Second Silesian War
1750–53	Voltaire joins Frederick's court in Prussia
Jan. 1756	Frederick and George II of England sign the Treaty of Westminster
Aug. 1756	Frederick invades Saxony; Seven Years' War begins
Oct. 1758	Frederick's sister Wilhelmina dies
Aug. 14, 1760	Prussians defeat the Austrians at Liegnitz
Oct. 1760	Russian and Austrian troops invade Berlin
Jan. 1762	Peter III succeeds Empress Elizabeth of Russia; he orders Russian troops to reverse their loyalties and fight for Prussia
Feb. 1763	Peace of Hubertusberg concludes Seven Years' War
1772	Austria, Prussia, and Russia partition Poland
1778–79	War of the Bavarian Succession
July 23, 1785	Frederick joins the League of Princes, an alliance of 14 states created to check Austrian expansionism
Aug. 17, 1786	Dies at Sans Souci

Index

America,   15, 17
Anhalt-Dessau, Leopold Maximilian von,   55, 56, 57, 63, 66, 70, 71
Anti-Machiavel,   59, 61
Austria,   15, 17, 33, 41, 44, 51, 55, 58, 59, 61, 63, 66, 67, 68, 71, 79, 89, 98, 99, 104
Austrian Netherlands,   42, 103
Bach, Carl Philipp Emanuel,   46
Bach, Johann Sebastian,   46, 47, 73
Bavaria,   32, 62, 63, 66, 67, 99, 101, 104
Beethoven, Ludwig van,   46
Belgium,   42
Berlin,   25, 31, 35, 39, 47, 71, 77, 80, 86, 87, 89, 91, 94, 103
Berlin Academy,   53
Berliner Singakademie,   47
Bohemia,   15, 19, 41, 61, 63, 66, 67, 69, 101
Bourbons,   17, 32
Breslau, Treaty of,   63, 67
Britain,   66, 69, 89
Burghausen,   101
Caesar, Julius,   26
Calvin, John,   27
Calvinism,   27, 28
Canada,   89, 99
Catherine II, empress of Russia,   95, 96, 98
Catt, Heinrich de,   85
Charles, prince of Lorraine,   63, 68, 69, 83
Charles VI, emperor of Austria,   41, 55
Charles VII, Holy Roman emperor,   58, 63, 66, 67
Charles Albert, elector of Bavaria *see* Charles VII
Chotusitz, Battle of,   63
Codex Fredericianus,   99
Crown Prince Cadets,   28
d'Alembert, Jean,   28
Daun, Leopold von,   19, 20, 80, 81, 83, 84, 87
de Chevert, Francois,   62
Dettingen, Battle of,   67
Diderot, Denis,   28
Diplomatic Revolution,   79
Doctor Akakia (Voltaire),   76
Dresden,   34, 35, 71, 80
Dresden, Peace of,   71

Duhan de Jandun, Jacques Egide,   26
Duties of Princes,   60
Elbe River,   80, 87
Elizabeth, empress of Russia,   15, 80, 89
Elizabeth Christina of Brunswick-Bevern (wife),   41, 43, 44
England,   15, 17, 28, 33, 39, 42, 51, 67, 79, 80, 83
Enlightenment,   28
Essay on a Method for Playing the Transverse Flute (Quantz),   46
Eugene, prince of Savoy,   44
Fasch, Carl Friedrich Christian,   46
Ferdinand, prince of Brunswick,   70
First Silesian War,   55, 56, 61, 62, 63, 64, 67
Fontenoy, Battle of,   67
Forms of Government,   60
France,   15, 17, 28, 32, 35, 36, 51, 58, 59, 65, 66, 67, 80, 89
Francis I, Holy Roman emperor,   69
Frankfurt,   37, 78
Frederick II Hohenzollern (Frederick the Great)
   author,   59, 60
   birth,   25
   death,   105
   early years,   25, 27, 28, 30
   education,   26
   Enlightenment philosophy and,   17, 28, 107
   First Silesian War and,   55, 56, 61, 62, 63
   king of Prussia,   51, 53, 54, 59, 64, 71, 73, 74, 79, 91, 92, 93, 94, 96, 99, 103, 107
   marriage,   41
   music and,   46, 74
   philosophy of rule,   59, 60, 61
   relationship with father,   25, 28, 29, 30, 34, 35, 36, 37, 38, 50
   Second Silesian War and,   65, 66, 67, 68, 69, 70, 71
   Seven Years' War and,   13–15, 17, 18, 20, 21, 23, 80, 81, 83, 84, 86, 87, 88, 89
   Voltaire and,   47, 71, 75, 76, 77, 78, 82, 103

Frederick, prince of Bayreuth (brother-in-law), 39

Frederick William, elector of Brandenburg (great-grandfather), 51

Frederick William I, king of Brandenburg-Prussia (father), 25, 26, 28, 29, 30, 31, 33, 34, 35, 36, 37, 39, 41, 42, 43, 46, 49, 50, 51, 53

Frederick William II, king of Prussia (nephew), 96

French Revolution, 28

Füssen, Peace of, 67

George I, king of England, 31

George II, king of England, 15, 31, 66, 67, 69, 83

Ghibellines, 33

Goethe, Johann Wolfgang von, 107

Graun, Carl Heinrich, 47

Graun, Johann Gottlieb, 47

Grenadier Guards, 51

Grumbkow, Friedrich Wilhelm von, 39, 41, 42

Guelphs, 32, 33

Habsburgs, 17, 31, 41, 42, 55, 58

Halle, University of, 53

Hanover, 31, 58, 104

Hanover, Convention of, 69

Herder, Johann Gottfried von, 106, 107

Hochkirch, 84, 85

Hohenfriedeberg, Battle of, 68, 69

Hohenzollern, Wilhelmina von (sister), 29, 31, 34, 35, 39, 47, 84

Holland, 35, 66, 67

Holy Roman Empire, 15, 31, 32, 55, 58, 66, 89

Hubertusburg, Treaty of, 89

Hume, David, 28

Hungary, 15, 41, 58

India, 15, 17, 89

Italy, 32, 42

Ivan VI, tsar of Russia, 95

Jacobite rebellion, 69

Joseph II, Holy Roman emperor, 96, 97, 99, 100, 101, 103

Katte, Hans Hermann von, 36, 37, 38, 44

Keith, Peter Karl Christoph von, 36, 37

Kesselsdorf, Battle of, 22, 70, 71

Khevenhüller, Ludwig Andreas, 62, 63

Klein-Schnellendorf, Convention of, 61, 63

Klopstock, Friedrich, 107

Kolin, Battle of, 19, 20, 80

Kunersdorf, Battle of, 15, 19, 86

Küstrin, 37, 38, 39, 43

Laudon, Gideon Ernst von, 19, 20, 86

League of Princes, 103

Leipzig, 77, 83

Lessing, Gotthold, 107

Leuthen, Battle of, 84

Liegnitz, Battle of, 13–15, 17, 18, 20, 21, 23, 86, 87

Lobositz, Battle of, 80

Louis XIV, king of France, 59, 67

Louis XV, king of France, 15, 75, 79, 80

Machiavelli, Niccolò, 59, 61

Manteuffel, Ernst Christoph, 48

Marcus Aurelius, 26

Maria Theresa, empress of Austria, 15, 20, 55, 56, 58, 59, 61, 63, 64, 66, 69, 70, 71, 79, 80, 89, 96, 98, 100, 103

Maupertuis, Pierre-Louis Moreau de, 76

Mithridate (Racine), 85

Mollwitz, Battle of, 56, 57, 80

Munich, 63

Musical Offering, The (Bach), 47

Neipperg, Wilhelm von, 56, 57, 61

Neuruppin, 43

Oder River, 51

Paris, 35

Paris, Treaty of, 66

Peter III, tsar of Russia, 89, 95

Philippsburg, 44

Pirna, Battle of, 80

Podewils, Heinrich von, 56

Poland, 13, 15, 19, 51, 68, 83, 84, 95, 97, 98, 99

Pomerania, 17, 51

"potato war" *see* War of the Bavarian Succession

Potsdam, 47, 78, 104

Pragmatic Sanction, 55, 58, 63

Prague, 61, 62, 67, 80, 81

Pressburg, 58

Prince, The (Machiavelli), 59

Quadruple Alliance, 67

Quantz, Johann Joachim, 46
Racine, Jean, 85
Rational Ideas on God, the World, the Soul of Man, and on All Things in General (Wolff), 53
Reflections on the Political Condition of Europe, 59
Regie, 99
Regis Iussu Cantio et Reliqua Canonica Arte Resoluta (Bach), 47
Rheinsberg, 46, 47, 48
Rhine River, 44, 51
Ritter, Gerhard, 61
Rochow, Friedrich von, 37
Rode, C. B., 105
Romania, 42
Rossbach, Battle of, 83
Rothenburg, Friedrich von, 35
Rousseau, Jean-Jacques, 28
Russia, 15, 79, 89, 91, 96, 98, 100
Saltykov, Peter, 86
Sans Souci, 71, 73, 75, 76, 77, 103, 104, 105
Sardinia, 67
Saxe, Maurice de, 44, 67
Saxony, 19, 22, 32, 34, 80, 81, 104
Schönhausen, 43
Schweidnitz, 88, 89
Schwerin, Kurt Christoph von, 56, 66, 80
Seckendorf, Ludwig Heinrich von, 41, 42
Second Silesian War, 65, 66, 67, 68, 69, 70, 71

Serbia, 42
Seven Years' War, 13–15, 17, 23, 80, 81, 83–89
Seydlitz, Friedrich von, 83
Silesia, 15, 32, 41, 51, 55, 56, 59, 61, 63, 65, 66, 69, 71, 86, 89, 94, 99, 100
Simon, Edith, 33
Soor, Battle of, 69
Sophia Dorothea, queen of Brandenburg-Prussia (mother), 25, 30, 31, 33, 34, 39, 82
Stuart, Charles Edward, 68, 69
Suhm, Ulrich Friedrich von, 48
Sweden, 15, 17, 89
Teschen, Peace of, 101
Thirty Years' War, 29
Torgau, Battle of, 87, 88
Turkey, 100
Union of Frankfurt, 66
Versailles, Treaty of, 80
Voltaire, 22, 47, 53, 71, 75, 76, 77, 78, 82, 86, 99, 103
Wallachia, 42
War of the Austrian Succession, 15, 22, 63, 66, 71
War of the Bavarian Succession, 99, 101
Westminster, Treaty of, 79
Wieland, Christoph, 107
Wolff, Christian von, 33
Worms, Treaty of, 67

Mary Kittredge was born in Pewaukee, Wisconsin, and educated at Trinity College in Connecticut. She is a writer of both fiction and nonfiction, and currently lives in North Branford, Connecticut.

Arthur M. Schlesinger, jr., taught history at Harvard for many years and is currently Albert Schweitzer Professor of the Humanities at City University of New York. He is the author of numerous highly praised works in American history and has twice been awarded the Pulitzer Prize. He served in the White House as special assistant to Presidents Kennedy and Johnson.